KEEPING NORTH EASTERN
STEAM ALIVE

NELPC

50

1966 - 2016

NORTH EASTERN LOCOMOTIVE PRESERVATION GROUP
KEEPING NORTH EASTERN STEAM ALIVE FOR FUTURE GENERATIONS

The three 'young men of vision' – Kevin Hudspith, Kevin Gould and Peter Proud – who conjured up the idea of saving examples of NER steam locomotives, which was the catalyst for the formation of the North Eastern Locomotive Preservation Group. NELPG members, past, present and future, in particular, and the heritage steam movement in general, have much to thank them for.

Their legacy, perpetuated by the Group's members and hard-working volunteers over the succeeding 50 years, is portrayed through the pages of this book, and is there for all to see in the NELPG's four locomotives, which have provided much pleasure to generations of people who have watched them, travelled behind them, or worked on them. In this last respect, the legacy has seen the perpetuation of specialist skills in steam locomotive overhaul, maintenance and operation, which, hopefully, can be passed on to future generations and, as this book proclaims in its title, helps to keep North Eastern steam alive. *John Hunt*

KEEPING NORTH EASTERN STEAM ALIVE

THE STORY OF FIFTY YEARS OF THE
NORTH EASTERN LOCOMOTIVE PRESERVATION GROUP

NELPC
50
1966 - 2016

SLP

Silver Link Publishing Ltd

First published in 2016

British Library Cataloguing in Publication Data

A catalogue record for this book is available from the British Library.

ISBN   978 185794 487 7 Limited Edition
        978 185794 483 9 Softcover Standard Edition

Silver Link Publishing Ltd
The Trundle
Ringstead Road
Great Addington
Kettering
Northants NN14 4BW

Tel/Fax: 01536 330588
email: sales@nostalgiacollection.com
Website: www.nostalgiacollection.com

Printed and bound in the Czech Republic

Half title: 'T2' No 2238, 'P3' No 2392 and 'K1' No 2005 bask in early morning sunshine inside Thornaby roundhouse on 22 December 1975 the last time steam locomotives were to use the roundhouse. *John Hunt*

Front endpaper: On a misty October day 'Q7' No 901 pilots 'P3' No 2392 through Northdale on the climb from Levisham towards Goathland. *Maurice Burns*

Below: 'T2' No 2238 leads 'P3' No 2392 and 'K1' No 2005 past Guisborough Junction at Middlesbrough en route from Thornaby to Grosmont on 22 December 1975, returning from the S&D 150 celebrations. *John Hunt*

Contents

Acknowledgements

This story of the 50 years of the North Eastern Locomotive Preservation Group has been compiled by John Hunt with the grateful and invaluable help of Maurice Burns, Nick Carter, Graham Holt, Chris Lawson, Ted Parker, Dave Pennock, Andrew Scott, Geoff Scurr, Richard Wheeler and Dave Whitfield. The team is also indebted to Richard Barber and David Dunn of the Armstrong Railway Photographic Trust, and picture contributors Bob Anderson, Michael Anderson, Roger Bastin, Andrew Bell, John Boyes, Maurice Burns, Darrin Crone, Mrs C. Davison, Gerry Dixon, Trevor Ermel, Chris Gammell, Bob Green, Richard Greenwood, J. W. Hague, Graham Holt, John Hunt, David Idle, Robin Lush, Pamela Marriner, Gavin Morrison, Les Nixon, Tom Noble, Ted Parker, Richard Pearson, Dave Pennock, Peter J. Robinson, Dave Rodgers, William Rogerson, Colin Smith, John Cooper Smith, Ken Snowdon, South Devon Railway, Brian Stephenson, Nigel Trotter, David Warren, Phil Waterfield and John Whiteley.

Unaccredited pictures are from the NELPG collection/archive.

FOREWORD BY
ANDREW SCOTT CBE, NELPG PRESIDENT

Fifty years ago, in a room above a pub in Newcastle, a motley collection of (mostly) young men came together over several pints of beer to decide what to do about something that concerned them greatly. Their backgrounds were diverse, but they were united by their fascination and passion for the steam locomotive – something that was rapidly disappearing from the scene. This was a mix of local people, from bank managers to shipyard workers, and of students, many of them incomers to Newcastle but all sharing a love of the steam railway. Everyone was aware of the very special heritage of steam in the North East. This was, after all, the place where the steam railway had originated around the time of the Battle of Waterloo. A century and a half after those first clumsy experiments, the steam locomotive continued to undertake, amongst other things, its original job of shifting coal from the mine to the riverside staiths from where it was shipped. Even in 1966, this scene was still part of everyday life on the banks of the Blyth, the Tyne and the Wear.

The engines that pulled the trains hadn't changed much, either. They were the North Eastern Railway's more or less standard six- and eight-wheeled mineral-hauling locomotives. In the early years of the 20th century they had been state-of-the-art and had continued to deliver the goods across North East England for 60 years. For most people they formed just part of the backdrop to everyday life, something to be taken for granted. Others, though, including everyone in that pub upstairs room, were captivated by the amazing spectacle of smoke and noise as the engines shifted coal and other goods between mine, factory and staith.

The roomful of activists shared something else that is often forgotten when people wonder just what made steam enthusiasts and trainspotters tick in their 1960s heyday. That was an awareness of rapid change in the world around us and of the consequential loss of things that, though we took them for granted, had shaped our very world. For some, such change was to be welcomed and embraced. Others were uneasy. Most felt they could do nothing about it. Yet all around them the evidence of the steam railway was disappearing. Hundred-ton locomotives – once the giants of the railway – arrived in Tyneside scrapyards and, within days, had been reduced to feedstock for the blast furnace. Our group in the pub that night had a niggling feeling that, whatever else they might feel, these changes should not go unmarked and it was up to them to act.

Since the Second World War Britain has been very good at monitoring and constraining change to buildings and landscape. We have systems for the listing of historically significant buildings and for protecting special landscapes. But when it comes to artefacts there are few controls. That's just the way it is and it was in this environment that our disparate group agreed that the loss of the steam locomotive as the diesel replaced it was something that should not happen. If no one else would do anything about it, then they would have to do something themselves. The idea of privately preserving a steam locomotive was launched.

And so it was that the North Eastern Locomotive Preservation Group was born. What was clear from day one was that if anything was to be achieved it would be through self-help. It's perhaps worth recalling that there was no Heritage Lottery Fund in 1966. There were no major private donors or public agencies waiting to help, and there wasn't much help from a railway industry that was focused on modernisation and on generating income from the scrap that change produced.

There wasn't much money, but there was determination and a sense – born out in practice – that if you want something enough, then determination would deliver. To raise the funds, members developed skills in publicity, fund-raising, marketing, publishing and negotiation. When we were successful, the emphasis shifted to locomotive overhaul, maintenance and, eventually, operating trains. Some brought their professional skills, others developed the skills and took them forward in their careers. Still more ran a double life – devoting their leisure hours to helping push forward an initiative totally different from the day job. Together they made it all happen.

Fifty years later, it is time to look back at the Group's own history. Today we own four locos, not just one, and we've played a part in the preservation, restoration and operation of several more. The NELPG's locos weren't the stars or the racehorses of the steam era. They were workaday engines that spent most of their time lumbering around the railway byways of the North East. But they were a crucial part of the history of the North East and they were unique. The collection is a hugely important part of North East England's heritage.

By now, the locos have been owned by the Group for longer than they were owned by the railway companies. The heritage operations they undertake – on the North Yorkshire Moors Railway, on the 'most beautiful railway in the world' from Fort William to Mallaig, and on visits to railways all over the UK, help new generations to understand both the appeal of the steam engine and the unique contribution it made to the shaping of today's world.

I've been proud to be a member of the NELPG since 1967. It's an organisation that just gets on with the job. Its continued ability to operate several locos at a time in different locations across the country marks it out as one of Britain's most successful voluntary railway preservation organisations. Every year brings more challenges as the world changes around the unchanging needs of our increasingly ancient locomotives. But if the NELPG's members can pass on to new generations the spirit that delivered the achievements so far, then the Group can go forward with confidence towards its centenary.

Andrew Scott CBE

Introduction – Friday 28 October 1966

1966 is best remembered, certainly by those with sporting interests, as the year that England won soccer's World Cup, an achievement that the national side has so far been unable to repeat! Harold Wilson was Prime Minister and, sadly, it was the year of the Aberfan disaster in South Wales, the mass funerals being held on 27 October. Britain had yet to join the European Community and decimal currency was still five years away. A three-bedroomed semi-detached house in the North East would have cost about £3,000, while the most popular car, a Ford Cortina, would have set you back about £750! A bottle of famous Newcastle Brown ale cost just 1s 9d (9p).

Newcastle United – and Sunderland – were in the First Division of the Football League and they met in a local derby at St James's Park on 29 October. In the week ending the 28th, Jim Reeves was top of the UK popular music chart with *Distant Drums*. Also in the Top 10 were the Four Tops, the Troggs, the Who, the Supremes and the Rolling Stones. These were the days of vinyl records, well before the advent of downloads on the internet, and the development of mobile phones and digital cameras.

In the North East, there was something particularly special about the final days of steam. Maybe it was the feeling of continuity from the days of the railway pioneers. Perhaps it was because many locos surviving locally had themselves been part of the scene for so long. Most of them were more than 50 years old. By 1967 they were the oldest engines still at work on BR, still providing the unglamorous yet essential service for which they had been designed so many years before.

Among the enthusiasts who gathered at the lineside in those final months of North East steam operation, there were some who felt that it was worth trying to save something of this part of our industrial heritage, and decided to do something about it. So it came to pass that the *Newcastle Evening Chronicle* of 26 October 1966 carried an article headlined 'They want to save old railway engines', which heralded the birth of the North Eastern Locomotive Preservation Group. This occurred two days later on the 28th, when the inaugural meeting was held in the Bridge Hotel, Newcastle, appropriately situated adjacent to Stephenson's High Level Bridge over the Tyne.

That night, 'young men of vision' met in an upstairs room in the Bridge Hotel, in the shadow of Stephenson's High Level Bridge at Newcastle. They comprised John Arnott Brown, Bob Anderson, Mick Denholm, Godfrey Valentine, J. Calderwood, Russell Wear, Dave Johnson, Alan Kane, J. Gallow, John Newbegin, Alan Wharram, John Shaw, Robin Dawe, Kevin Gould, Chris Smyth, Peter Proud, Neville Stead, Richard Wheeler and Kevin Hudspith. How many of them made a nostalgic return to the Bridge Hotel on 28 October 2016?

That fateful evening a vote was taken as to which locomotive should be the subject of fund-raising; of the 19 present, 11 opted for a 'J27', five favoured a 'Q6', and three suggested either. The 'J27' was therefore selected, not necessarily because it was the more popular one, but because it was the cheaper to buy! At this first meeting, with little idea of how it was to be achieved, they resolved to attempt to purchase a locomotive. So the die was cast, and fund-raising started there and then. After paying for the hire of the room, the 'fund' stood at 5s 6d (27½p)!

It was Kevin Hudspith, Peter Proud and Kevin Gould who can be credited with the foresight in calling that historic first meeting and thus creating the North

Eastern Locomotive Preservation Group. What they, and those early pioneer preservationists, cannot possibly have foreseen were the subsequent events and achievements of the ensuing 50 years, chronicled in the pages of this book. NELPG members, past, present and future, and the railway preservation world in general, have much to thank them for.

So, the foundation was laid of an organisation that was to exceed the expectations of its first members.

The enthusiasm then aroused led to a second meeting held at the Express Hotel, Westgate Road, Newcastle, in the shadow of the statue of railway pioneer George Stephenson, on 18 November. From these humble beginnings an unforgettable euphoria was generated, and with driving enthusiasm and the essential attributes of initiative, ingenuity and determination, success seemed assured!

The headline that appeared in the Newcastle Evening Chronicle on 26th October 1966.

The Bridge Hotel, Newcastle, situated between the Tyne Bridge and, on the right, Stephenson's historic High Level road and rail bridge. *John Hunt*

The North East of England had been the cradle of railways. They enabled the exploitation of the rich seams of coal that were to establish an economy and a way of life that made the North East great. Here, men like William Hedley and George Stephenson built the world's first locomotives in the opening years of the 19th century. Their job was to haul trains of coal from the collieries down to the banks of the Tyne, Wear and Tees, where it could be loaded into ships. The steam locomotive went on to provide transport for the world, and 150 years later, as the end of the steam era approached, some of the last steam locos in Britain were still to be found at work serving the collieries of Northumberland and Durham.

During the 19th century a dense network of railways developed in Northumberland, Durham and the Cleveland area of north Yorkshire to serve industry

the 19th century, inevitably brought consolidation, and the North Eastern Railway (NER) emerged with a near monopoly.

From its North Road works at Darlington came a long line of distinguished locomotives, not least the Raven 'Atlantics', but also a host of unpretentious, workaday locomotives designed to transport the very lifeblood of the North East – coal, iron and steel. The NER's requirements for its coal and mineral engines were straightforward – no-nonsense power and lots of it! By the time of the First World War these requirements were being met by two distinct types of loco – six- and eight-coupled tender engines – examples of which were to survive until the end of BR steam operations in the area. These were the 'P3' Class 0-6-0s (referred to by the London & North Eastern Railway [LNER] and BR as 'J27') and the 'T2' (later

An official NER works photograph of 'P3' No 2338.

and the communities associated with it. Hundreds of coal mines and scores of quarries supplied the raw materials for the North East's steelworks, factories and power stations. Coal in vast quantities was taken by sea from ports on the area's river estuaries to fuel industry at home and abroad. The resultant railway mania and proliferation of new railway lines throughout

'Q6') Class 0-8-0s. The North Eastern Locomotive Preservation Group was to preserve an example of each, and it is these that were to form the basis of the Group's collection.

The 'P3' was the largest of the North Eastern Railway 0-6-0 classes. They were hardworking engines, and 115 were built between 1906 and 1923. It was

An official NER works photograph of 'T2' No 1247.

Complete with miniature snowplough, 'T2' No 63395 passes through Bensham as it climbs up from Norwood Junction to Gateshead with coal empties on 2 March 1967. *Trevor Ermel*

In 1966 steam could be seen throughout the North Eastern Region, and this was a typical scene in York shed's roundhouse (now the NRM) on 16 August, with 'K1' No 62028, BR Standard No 77012, 'V2' No 60806, 'WD' No 90347, 9F No 92239 and 'J27' No 65894 on view. *Roger Bastin*

the final development of a series of 0-6-0s with small wheels and ever-larger boilers. These were ideal for the relatively low speeds and short distances covered by much of the company's colliery traffic. They were designed by Wilson Worsdell, the NER's Chief Mechanical Engineer, and were introduced in 1906. The huge, 5ft 6in-diameter boiler applied to the 'P3' and its predecessor, the 'P2', was a major innovation and was the key to the locomotive's ability to handle heavy loads of coal on the company's steeply graded routes. The type was to be a familiar sight in the North East for more than 60 years.

Alongside them worked Class 'T2' 0-8-0s, 120 of which were built by the NER between 1913 and 1921 for working heavy coal traffic. Designed by Vincent Raven, these powerful and elegant engines were built with superheated boilers and steam reversing gear, and, not surprisingly, were popular with drivers and firemen all over the system.

By 1966, as British Railways classes 'J27' and 'Q6' respectively, they were the last pre-Grouping (1923) locomotives in Britain, and only a handful of representatives of each class had survived the closures of lines and pits, and the march of dieselisation. Their time was now fast running out, and it was clear that these locomotives would soon be withdrawn from service.

There were 28 'J27s' in service when the NELPG was formed on 28 October 1966, these being concentrated at both North and South Blyth and at Sunderland. By 31 January 1967 there were just 21. In that three-month period members began to get used to the NELPG's first Treasurer, Kevin Hudspith, saying in his broad Geordie accent, 'The fund noo stands at…', but, after three months, the figure he announced was only £108 in total. The burgeoning sales initiative, however, was beginning to make a huge difference to Kevin's fund, which gained in strength as a result.

Another key stepping stone in the NELPG's development was joining the Association of Railway Preservation Societies (ARPS) as a full member.

This was an umbrella organisation for locomotive and railway preservation societies, one of its prime functions being to ensure that all societies had constitutions and were correctly run. ARPS membership was later to have hugely significant implications, not only in saving the 'J27', but also the 'Q6'. We also quickly learned that friendships with other like-minded societies paid huge dividends.

Back on the ground, steam in the North East was originally scheduled to finish in June 1967. Had this been achieved, it is doubtful whether either a 'J27' or 'Q6' would have been saved, as at that time the NELPG fund totalled just £550 against the £1,400 needed to buy a 'J27'.

Above and right: If it were not for the NELPG, this is the fate that would have befallen the 'J27' and the 'Q6'. Examples of less fortunate classmates are reduced to scrap at Ellis Metals, Tyneside – No 63427 above and No 65794 right. *Trevor Ermel/Armstrong Trust*

Between 1 February and the end of June 1967, 12 'J27's were withdrawn, five from South Blyth and seven from Sunderland. Only one of the type survived at Sunderland, No 65894, which had moved there from York on 2 October 1966. BR then decided to concentrate all the last 'J27's at Sunderland, and Nos 65789, 65795, 65855, 65860, 65879 and 65882 were transferred from South Blyth, and Nos 65804, 65811 and 65892 from North Blyth. On 28 May 1967 the last 'J27' left South Blyth as the shed closed to steam. With it came the end of a 60-year era of 'J27s' working in the Northumberland coalfields.

All 'J27s' at that time had done in excess of 60,000 miles of hard work since their last major overhaul and, with Darlington Works being long closed, there were no overhaul facilities, or even spare parts, unless they could be removed from condemned engines. With knocking axle boxes and big ends, and rattling side rods, the rugged 'J27s' worked on, helped by their well-designed saturated boilers that required little maintenance. The final three months in traffic saw no easing off of the type of work they did. They still flogged up the steep gradients to collieries, then took 500-ton loose-coupled coal trains to power stations or coal staiths for onward shipment. The friendly crews at Sunderland allowed any enthusiast who asked for a footplate ride to 'come on up' and this closeness to the engines and the friendly people of the North East certainly played a part in enthusiasts contributing to the appeal fund.

As the very end approached, and the fund was nearing its objective, it was decided to have a look at which 'J27' should be our target. It would have been ideal to preserve one of the original engines built in 1906 by the NER, such as No 65795, which was still working in early July 1967 after an amazing 61 years of service. This would certainly have been the engine to preserve, but an engine could be in traffic one day, withdrawn the next, then sold and delivered to a scrapyard in eight weeks. No 65795 suffered just that fate and was cut up and gone forever by September 1967.

Of the five last operational 'J27s', therefore, the choice of which to preserve was not easy. No 65811 had been built by the North British Locomotive Company in Glasgow in 1908, No 65855 by Beyer Peacock, also in 1908, and Nos 65879, 65882 and 65894 were all built at North Road, Darlington, in 1922 or 1923. The latter three had the advantage of being built in Darlington but had the disadvantage that they had been built with a superheated boiler (with a huge smokebox) and piston valves, rather than the saturated boiler and slide valves of the original design. All three had been refitted with a spare saturated boiler towards the end of their working lives, with the rather unsightly frame extension for the superheated boiler still visible. Some members favoured No 65811 as a slide valve version, but the Committee decided, after weighing up all the factors, to go for No 65894 as the best of the three Darlington engines left, mainly

because its boiler was built in 1958 and had given no maintenance problems. With No 65894 selected, but still in BR everyday traffic, one Committee member travelled from Teesside to have an unusual experience he will never forget, that of a cab ride on No 65894 on the Silksworth branch while on his way to a Newcastle meeting to preserve it!

Steam struggled on until 9 September, but even then NELPG funds were only £911 towards the £1,400 required. Fortunately the purchase process allowed more vital days to raise more money. By 1 October 1967, with time seriously running out, the fund had reached £1,100, only £300 short. However, with purchase hopefully imminent, and the engine moved to Tyne Dock's old wagon works for safe keeping, a body blow was received when BR raised the purchase price to £1,800, reflecting a surge in the world value of copper; the shortfall was now £700! The copper price increase affected lots of potential steam engine purchases throughout the growing preservation movement. After consultation between NELPG Chairman Bryce Greenfield and ARPS Chairman Peter Manisty, the latter decided to ask BR for a bulk purchase deal for many locomotives, of which No 65894 was just one. By joining with potential owners at Carnforth and the Severn Valley Railway, the Peter Manisty bulk purchase deal saw the 'J27' price discounted back to £1,400 – a huge achievement that brought much relief.

The first AGM of the Group, held on 3 November, was a momentous occasion, attended by more than 70 members. The Chairman, Bryce Greenfield, reported on the Group's first year, a year in which membership

Bryce Greenfield, first Chairman of the NELPG, in the cab of one of his beloved 'A3s', No 2599 *Book Law*, in 1938, and (below) the cheque that purchased the 'J27'.

had reached more than 200, and £1,400 had been raised to purchase a 'J27'. Not all the promised cash had been received, however, and to ensure that the purchase could go ahead, unknown to members, a £100 overdraft had been arranged with the bank, for which Bryce had to lodge personal security as guarantees. Retiring Treasurer Kevin Hudspith was

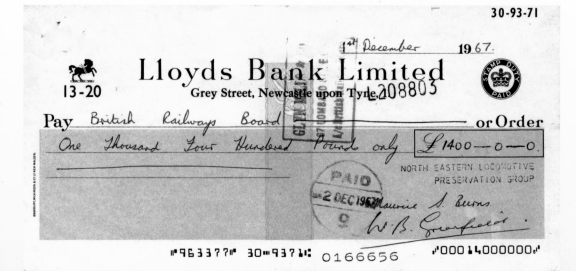

No 65894, with superheated boiler, stands next to the mechanical coaling plant at York depot in 1962. *Nigel Trotter*

No 65894, still with its superheated boiler, passes southbound on the East Coast Main Line at Thirsk with a very lengthy train of mineral wagons. *J.W. Hague/NERA Collection*

Following its visit to North Road Works in 1963, No 65894 was fitted with a saturated boiler and is pictured inside York roundhouse shortly after its return from Darlington. *Nigel Trotter*

warmly thanked for his efforts with 'the fund' and was succeeded by Maurice Burns. One of his first tasks was to write out the cheque to purchase No 65894. Having witnessed so many engines being cut up for scrap, to be writing out the cheque that would save one was immensely satisfying. With volunteers in jubilant mood, it was subsequently countersigned by Bryce Greenfield, using No 65894's running plate as a writing desk. It had been a long, hard struggle, but we had done it, and the last 'J27' became NELPG property on 1 December 1967. 10% of the purchase price came from membership subscriptions, 60% from donations and a vital 30% from sales. In the event the overdraft was not needed, which was a good job, as failure to repay it by 31 December would have resulted in an interest charge of 16%!

The 'J27' we preserved

No 65894, as 'P3' No 2392, had first entered service on 19 September 1923, being the last engine delivered of the last batch of this class, in an order for ten engines that had been placed on 14 December 1922. Like many locomotives turned out from the Darlington North Road Works, it was allocated to Darlington shed to be run in. Very soon it was transferred to Ferryhill, from which shed it worked trains in the South Durham coalfield until 1930. At this time it was transferred to York and worked local goods trains over a number of routes, including the lines to Scarborough and Whitby.

Life continued uneventfully until 21 November 1938 when, in bad weather while crossing the main line at York from Branches Yard to the Scarborough line, it was run into by 'B16' No 2363. No 2392 was knocked over on to its side and suffered considerable damage. The 'B16' was only slightly damaged, but nevertheless, after some delay, both locomotives were moved to Darlington Works. At one stage it seemed likely that No 2392 would be broken up, but the international situation of early 1939 led to a number of locomotives being reinstated that, in earlier times, might have been written off. Luckily No 2392 was reprieved and repairs were carried out, including probably new frames.

It remained at York until 1943, when a major reallocation of locomotives took place, and No 2392 was moved to Neville Hill, Leeds. Three years later it was renumbered No 5894 as part of Thompson's renumbering scheme. In 1950, or thereabouts, it returned to York, and in 1951 it was renumbered 65894 in the BR series, being almost the last 'J27' to receive its new number.

No 65894 spent almost all of its BR career at York, one of only a few of this class allocated there during this period. Its duties were on local freight turns (including on the York Foss Islands branch), as pilot in the York Engineers Yard, as an occasional snowplough engine, and at times as shed pilot. It also worked the last pick-up goods on the Ryedale line before closure in August 1964. In comparison with its fellow 'J27s' working in Northumberland and Durham, No 65894 saw little exertion, a fact taken into consideration

Before it and its fellow 'J27s' received the cleaning attentions of enthusiasts, No 65894 stands inside Sunderland South Dock roundhouse on 1 March 1967. *Graham Holt*

when it was selected for preservation. In March 1963 it visited Darlington Works for overhaul, when it was fitted with its non-superheated boiler, which thus saw only four years use before withdrawal.

As a finale to its BR career, with the end of steam in the North East approaching, No 65894 was transferred to Sunderland on 2 October 1966 to reinforce the diminishing fleet of 'J27s' working coal trains in East Durham. Over the next 11 months, the engine became a great favourite with enthusiasts as it worked trains on such spectacular routes as the 1 in 45 Seaton Bank and the similarly graded Silksworth

Colliery branch. On 8 September 1967 No 65894 worked the last steam turn, the famous 'Blue Star Special', up the Silksworth branch with coal empties, and on the following day worked the last turn from Sunderland to South Hetton colliery. Following withdrawal, No 65894 was moved to Tyne Dock MPD, together with a number of other locomotives awaiting disposal for scrap, but was to become the only 'J27' to survive. With now not a penny left in the bank and the last 'Q6' No 63395 also in store at Tyne Dock, somehow it also had to be saved…

After the cleaning sessions, No 65894 keeps company with fellow 'J27s' Nos 65855, 65811 and 65879 inside Sunderland South Dock roundhouse in August 1967. *Maurice Burns*

Looking superb after being cleaned by enthusiasts, No 65894 climbs Seaton bank, bound for South Hetton colliery during the final week of steam operation in September 1967. *Maurice Burns*

No 65894 heads south at Ryhope silhouetted against the North Sea on 8 September 1967, the penultimate day of steam traction on BR in the North East. *John Hunt*

On the final day of steam on the Silksworth branch, No 65894, suitably adorned with a 'North Eastern Steam Farewell' headboard and the famous blue star to reflect the Newcastle Brown Ale drinking habits of some of the photographers, heads coal empties up towards the colliery. In the background, Peter Proud attempts to chase the train on foot! *John Hunt*

3 No 63395 –
THE GREAT SURVIVOR

Twenty-four 'Q6s' were in traffic when the NELPG was founded in October 1966, but as time progressed they were gradually withdrawn from service and sold to local scrap dealers for cutting up. In the three months to 31 January 1967 withdrawals at Tyne Dock, Sunderland and Hartlepool left just 17 'Q6s', and by the original planned finishing date of

In respectable external condition, No 63395 crosses the River Wear at Monkwearmouth with a southbound coal train on 29 August 1967. *Brian Stephenson*

June 1967 they were down to just 11 – but still the survivors were working flat out every day. Tyne Dock withdrew its last two 'Q6s' on 1 July, leaving just four – Nos 63431, 63344, and 63387 at Hartlepool, and a solitary No 63395 at Sunderland.

While at that time the NELPG clearly had no money for a 'Q6', members could still dream: if we had some money, which engine would we buy? All remaining 'Q6s', like the 'J27s', were in quite an appalling condition, having run at least 60,000 miles in heavy use since their last major overhauls. Cleaning of some engines by enthusiasts often gave a rosy-

Seen during the months before it was cleaned by enthusiasts, a woebegone No 63395 climbs Seaton Bank with empties for South Hetton colliery in February 1967. *Maurice Burns*

coloured view of what the engines were really like! On the last day of operation, 9 September 1967, there were just two operational 'Q6s' left out of the 120 engines originally built. These were No 63387 at Hartlepool and No 63395 at Sunderland. There was no expert inspection made of these two engines, but it was decided to try and have one locomotive put aside – and the chosen engine was No 63395. This was partly because it had undergone a Darlington North Road intermediate overhaul in September 1965. Nearly as important, it was a favourite engine with enthusiasts, who had unofficially cleaned it and taken many photographs with black smoke arranged by the helpful crews. However, six months prior to withdrawal No 63395 was steaming so badly that one very fit photographer, taking pictures of the locomotive climbing the 1 in 40 Seaton Bank, was able to outrun it, as it was going so slowly – taking 11 pictures in the process! Shed boilersmiths then did a works job of a substantial re-tubing, replacing 97 small tubes to keep No 63395 in traffic a little longer. In truth though,

No 63395 was in very poor condition, but was still rostered six days out of seven, covering more than 1,000 miles a week. Unknown to NELPG members, however, No 63395 had been running with a serious hidden defect. There was a fracture in the front tube plate, hidden behind the superheater header, which, if it had been found by the boiler inspector, would have seen it instantly withdrawn and scrapped, leaving only No 63387 to be preserved.

In the meantime, good contacts had been established with the regional BR engineering managers at Newcastle, many of whom had a soft spot for steam, even though these same men were responsible for eliminating it! One of these was John Bellwood, Traction Engineer for the North Eastern Region, who at the time was himself involved with preservation at the infant Keighley & Worth Valley Railway. John had earlier been responsible for the transfer of two 'J72' engines, Nos 69005 and 69023, into Departmental service in October 1964 as Nos 58 and 59. At first they were used to defrost points and coal wagons

on the staiths at Blyth – a reason many believed
he totally made up in order to gain time for their
preservation. Eventually they were stored at Heaton
for a long period before No 58 was moved to Tyne
Dock's old wagon works (No 59 had by then been
bought privately for preservation). John allowed Nos
65894 and 63395 to join it until June 1968, pending the
hoped-for purchase of the 'Q6' for a quoted price of
£2,100.

With the 'J27' secured, the appeal for donations
to save the last 'Q6' was launched in early December
1967, but news of this appeal by national publicity in
The Railway Magazine and *Railway World* could not be
in place until January 1968. After the high of finally
purchasing No 65894, we then received a body blow.
Maurice Burns received an unexpected phone call
from Bryce Greenfield, which opened with, 'We have
had a letter from BR. You have had it, Maurice. 63395 is
going for scrap.' In shock, Bryce, a through and through
LNER fan, read out the BR letter dated 5 December
1967 that starkly said: 'Locomotive No 63395, together
with other locomotives, has been disposed of by
competitive tender and I regret it is not now available
for offer to you.'

Remember, this was a time when BR contracts
with scrapyards expressly forbade resale to anyone,
never mind railway enthusiasts. The news came as a
staggering blow, particularly in the light of previous
assurances. Worse was to follow. On the day
following receipt of the letter, Secretary Neville Stead,
accompanied by Richard Wheeler, talked his way into
the Managing Director's office at Clayton & Davy's
scrapyard in Dunston, as they were thought to be the
likely purchaser. Mr Davy assured them that he was not
the purchaser of No 63395, but he was able to find out
that the locomotive had been sold to Hughes Bolckow
Ltd at Blyth. It was scheduled to be towed from what
was thought to have been the safe haven of Tyne Dock
to Bolckow's scrapyard the next day. Then, to the
surprise and delight of Group members, the diesel
loco crew rostered to accompany the engine did not
report for duty that day. Many theories exist as to why
this happened, a number suggesting that the famous
Newcastle Brown Ale may have played a significant
role, but it is more likely that John Bellwood, who was
central to the engine being put aside, had intervened,
phoned the shed master and cancelled the job to allow
time for the NELPG Committee to find a way forward.

Within 24 hours the Group held an emergency
Committee meeting to explore all avenues to save No
63395. Next day Neville Stead virtually camped at the
Hughes Bolckow scrapyard, waiting for the Managing
Director to arrive, and badgered him for a meeting to
discuss the situation. Bryce Greenfield, a former Major
in the Army, accompanied Neville to the meeting.
Hughes Bolckow was well used to enthusiasts visiting
its scrapyard, but never before had they wanted to
buy a locomotive. The Managing Director was soon

convinced of our passion to save No 63395, the very
last steam engine to be bought by the scrapyard, but he
was unable to resell because of the ban on resale in his
BR purchase contract. This was a standard condition
applicable to all scrap dealers in the UK, which also
applied to the hundreds of engines in Dai Woodham's
scrapyard at Barry in South Wales. So how could a
small preservation society, with only a few hundred
members, change the British Railways Board (BRB)
policy? Little chance?

But we weren't on our own. Bryce Greenfield
had, during the bulk purchasing negotiation to reduce
the price of No 65894, formed an excellent working
relationship with ARPS Chairman Peter Manisty.
In discussions, Peter said it would be better if a
representative of all societies made an approach to
the BRB rather than just one small society. In mid-
December 1967 Peter set up a meeting with the
BRB, with a result for which the entire preservation
movement should be thankful. Peter liked a challenge
and came out of the meeting having changed the
standard terms and conditions of the BRB sales
contract – a truly amazing feat. Engines for the very
first time could now be resold to preservation groups.
It was a breakthrough initiated by the NELPG that
allowed a real chance not just to save No 63395, but
for other preservationists to go on and purchase the
200 locomotives at Barry.

No 63395 still remained at Tyne Dock as further
meetings with Hughes Bolckow took place, and a deal
was finally stuck whereby the scrapyard would be given
£200 more than the £2,100 they paid for the engine,
thereby guaranteeing their otherwise lost profit, and
stage payments were agreed, with the total price of
£2,300 to be raised in five months.

The enormity of this task cannot be overestimated.
It had taken a full 12 months for the NELPG to raise
the £1,400 to save No 65894, and the Group now had
just five months to raise £2,300. If this was not hard
enough, several other preservation societies were
making similar appeals elsewhere for their schemes.
Societies such as the B1 Locomotive Society, seeking
to save No 61306, and the A2 Preservation Society,
wanting to save No 60532 *Blue Peter*, were struggling
so badly, and were so likely to fail, that they had
appealed to the ARPS, and Peter Manisty in particular,
for help. It was also about this time that the North
Eastern Class 'J21' No 65033, which we all thought
was secure on the BRB approved list for preservation,
was suddenly removed from it and was to be sold for
scrap. Only through the intervention of Frank Atkinson,
who was developing the Beamish Open Air Museum,
was an appeal launched to save the engine, but this, of
course, was seeking money from the same enthusiasts
that we were. In the event, the 'J21' was saved just five
days before it was to be towed away for scrap. 'J72' No
69023 had been purchased privately by Ron Ainsworth,
so was also saved. By contrast, No 69005, which was

stored at Tyne Dock and which it was thought could not be moved because it was blocked in behind Nos 63395 and 65894, was extracted by the shed staff, who moved all the engines one weekday, and was taken away for scrap. When our volunteers arrived the following Sunday, an engine that could perhaps have been saved for just £400 was gone forever.

It was against this uncertain background, where things could change on a daily basis, that the NELPG was trying to raise the then enormous sum of £2,300. Drastic action was required, so an emergency newsletter was sent out appealing for donations and calling an Extraordinary General Meeting (EGM) to decide what course of action to take: borrow the money, abandon the project, or raise as much money as possible and borrow the balance.

Inevitably it was the latter course of action that was approved, and members rose to the challenge magnificently. The reaction was unprecedented: from £464 on 31 December, the fund had risen to £1,316 by 5 January 1968, a fantastic response to the appeal. But how was such an increase possible in just five days? Not reported all those years ago was that, immediately before the meeting, Bryce Greenfield and Maurice Burns took influential member Brian Hollingsworth out for a drink and explained our plight. The atmosphere at the EGM was full of enthusiasm and passion to save No 63395, and at the end Brian Hollingsworth, swept along with the spirit of the meeting, handed Maurice a cheque for £500. It was an amazing donation at just the right time. The Group's efforts were further encouraged by the news that Hughes Bolckow was prepared to accept a deposit of £1,200, with the balance due on 31 March. At the same time, the appeal in the railway press had clearly caught enthusiasts' imagination as the post delivered donation after donation to the fund. Thus

THE LAST PRE-GROUPING LOCOMOTIVE

to work on British Railways, "Q6" 0-8-0 No. 63395 exerted a strong pull on both coal trains **AND** railway enthusiasts.

900-ton loads brought up the 1 in 50 gradient of the Hylton Castle Branch, attracted many thousands of photographers to North East Durham during the last months of steam operation.

The engine, built 1918, is in magnificent condition but now stands out of steam awaiting your decision? £1,000 must be raised within 3 months, so on your action the future of this engine will depend. Which is it to be—

PRESERVATION or to the **SCRAPYARDS? ? ?**
It is up to YOU to decide

Please send YOUR donation to:—Q6 Appeal, North Eastern Locomotive Preservation Group, 2 Highfield Gardens, Eaglescliffe, Co. Durham, and help buy a working stablemate for J27 No. 65894.

on 1 April the Committee was able to report that No 63395 had been purchased for the sum of £2,300, a total that had nearly been raised in full. Member Derek Marshall had offered NELPG a temporary loan of £500, but, in the event, Peter J. Robinson, Treasurer, loaned his life savings of £150 to cover the necessary cheque until the subsequent receipt of appeal monies to secure the ownership of No 63395. As this story indicates, No 63395 is a true survivor. It was the last engine Hughes Bolckow bought for scrap, but an engine that never arrived at its yard – a tribute to all the enthusiasts who rose to the challenge to secure its future.

WD	2-8-0	90414	88 - 12 - 0	£1945	0 0	4/11/67		WEST
WD	2-8-0	90418	88 - 12 - 0	£1945	0 0	29-10-67		HARTLEPOOL
WD	2-8-0	90627	88 - 12 - 0	£1945	0 0	29-10-67		''
WD	2-8-0	90644	88 - 12 - 0	£1945	0 0	29-10-67		''
WD	2-8-0	90695	88 - 12 - 0	£1945	0 0	29-10-67		''
Q6*	0-8-0	63395	80 - 15 - 3	£2100	0 0			TYNE DOCK

* RE-SOLD N.E.L.P.G

This most significant image of the very last page of the Hughes Bolckow scrapyard list shows the last engine they bought as No 63395. The columns indicate loco type, number, weight, price paid, date received at the scrap yard and which loco shed it came from. Thanks to enthusiasts, the date received for No 63395 is blank.

Telephone: **BLYTH 3666**
Telegrams: "Battleships Blyth"

INVOICE

No. X. 2301

BATTLESHIP WHARF,

Major W.B. Greenfield, M.B.E.   **BLYTH,**............30th January,................19 68

M   North Eastern Locomotive Preservation Group,
    104 Dryden Road,
    GATESHEAD, on TYNE 9,
    Co. Durham.

Dr. to   HUGHES BOLCKOW LIMITED.

(MEMBER OF THE METAL INDUSTRIES GROUP OF COMPANIES)

Your Order No........................   Issue Instruction No............................

	Description			Unit Price	Total
to	B.R. Locomotive No. 63395, class Q6.				£2,300. -.
					CHEQUE FOR £1,200. ALREAD RECEIVED.

The NELPG Chairman Major Bryce Greenfield MBE was justifiably proud when he received this receipt from Hughes Bolckow for the £1,200 deposit against the full invoiced price to save No 63395.

The 'Q6' we preserved

No 63395 was completed as 'T2' No 2238 by the North Eastern Railway at its Darlington North Road Works on 2 December 1918, one of eight built in that year. It was a special order authorised by the War Office to replace locomotives sent to France to assist the war effort. In the 'T2', Vincent Raven produced an engine that could be driven 'all out' – full regulator and full forward gear – for indefinite periods at anything up to mineral train speeds. In 1915 examples of the class had undergone dynamometer trials on 700-ton trains between Newport and Shildon in County Durham, putting up some impressive performances and comparing very favourably with the then newly introduced electric locomotives working that line. The 'T2s', or 'Q6s' as they were later classified by the LNER and BR, proved to be extremely successful engines, carrying on a fine North Eastern Railway tradition for freight haulage. As a measure of their success, the basic design of the locomotive was never altered, though some engines, including No 63395, gave up their self-trimming tenders to the famous NER three-cylinder 'Atlantics', in exchange for conventional ones.

Following completion, No 2238 was sent to Gateshead for running in and allocation to Blaydon depot. There it remained for 25 years before beginning extensive travels throughout the North East. Sojourns at Newport, Darlington, West Hartlepool and Hull Dairycoates preceded a long spell allocated to Selby depot from 1 December 1949. On 14 June 1959 No 63395 was transferred once more to Darlington, then to Consett, before it was finally sent to Sunderland South Dock on 23 May 1965. From there the 'Q6' worked south to Seaham, Teesside and South Hetton and northwards to the Tyne until, as one of the last 'Q6s' in service, it embarked upon its journey into preservation after working the last steam-hauled coal train from Vane Tempest colliery, Seaham, on 9 September 1967.

The Group's 'Q6', as NER 'T2' No 2238, heads a long eastbound coal train at Wylam on the Carlisle-Newcastle line in the 1920s. *J. W. Armstrong/Armstrong Trust*

In this iconic image, 'Q6' No 63395, displaying the cleaning efforts of the photographer and friends, makes a superb sight tackling the start of the 1 in 40 of Seaton Bank at Ryhope in September 1967. It was sights such as this that encouraged the fantastic response to the NELPG's fund-raising appeals. *Maurice Burns*

A chance meeting on a train from York to Newcastle one Sunday evening early in 1966 led to a link between members of Newcastle University Railway Society (NURS) and a number of Tyneside enthusiasts who regularly met in the refreshment room of Newcastle Central station's island platform on Friday evenings. It was during one of these gatherings that those present were asked if they would be prepared to commit to a weekly contribution of perhaps 2s 6d (12.5p) towards the preservation of one of the ex-North Eastern Railway locomotives that were still to be seen passing through the station.

Once the NELPG had formally come into being, fund-raising started in earnest, but it was painfully slow. After three months the sum raised amounted to £108 in total. The first Committee had never done anything

The top picture shows an auction of railwayana presided over by John Hunt and Ian Storey, while the sales team of Peter Woodhouse, Richard Wheeler and Chris Lawson are busy in the Bridge Hotel in 1972.

like this before, so it took a little while to get a grip of things. News items and adverts in the local and railway press raised the fund profile, but money was tight and there were many appeals for more glamorous locomotives than a rusty freight-hauling 'J27', even if it was one of the last pre-1923 Grouping locomotives still working. NURS members played a major part in raising funds by establishing an active sales team. Large quantities of photographs were printed by members for sale to enthusiasts. Members travelled on railtours all over the North specifically to raise funds from sales and from raffles, with the kind forbearance of the tour promoters, and took sales stands to model railway exhibitions and other events.

The first NELPG secretary, Neville Stead, had raised a significant amount of money by producing a 5/- booklet (25p), 'Tyneside Steam', advising visiting enthusiasts of the best places to go to see and photograph the remaining North Eastern steam locos. When these engines were finally withdrawn in September 1967, NURS members researched and published booklets giving similar information about the remaining industrial steam locos, predominantly in colliery use, first in Northumberland and Durham, then in Yorkshire and North West England. Many hours were spent checking information on the ground, typing wax

stencils with two fingers, printing thousands of sheets on a school's Gestetner duplicator, collating the pages, and stapling the finished booklets. With assistance from other enthusiasts, further booklets were produced to guide visitors to see the remaining main-line steam locomotives in Western Europe, including Austria, Germany, France, Italy, Spain and Portugal. A change to professional printing eased the production process and resulted in a much more presentable product. In the end, thousands were sold, making a very real contribution to funds. A few examples of these duplicated booklets are shown below.

NURS members also organised a series of public film shows at the University and the Tyneside Film Theatre, showing documentaries hired from the British Transport Film Unit and rail-themed feature films. These attracted large audiences, raising valuable income and increasing public awareness of the NELPG.

Fifty years later, the current President, Chairman, Secretary and Treasurer of NELPG are all former members of the NURS, which brought them together in the late 1960s. Some might have achieved better examination results if they had spent less time on their hobby, but I doubt any would now regret how they chose to spend their time!

For the first ten years of the Group's existence, the vast bulk of its income to buy, overhaul and maintain its locomotives resulted from donations and sales. The value of sales to the Group was hugely boosted by the creativity of members. Publications, photographs, original artworks, specially commissioned T-shirts and badges, a sound cassette of the Group's locomotives at work, all made more money than simply retailing commercial products.

After the Shildon celebrations of 1975, which saw perhaps the pinnacle of retail sales, income from locomotive operations became the increasingly dominant source of funds, with railtours also making an increasingly significant contribution.

Looking back, it seems remarkable that a fleet of three NELPG-owned locomotives was established and restored almost entirely as a result of individual members dipping their hands into their pockets, sometimes in return for an NELPG-published book or souvenir, or just as often for no hope of a return other than the knowledge that the Group's locomotives would survive to operate again.

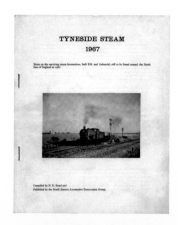

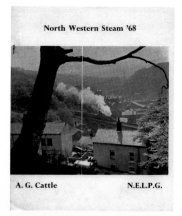

Manning a sales stall – or rather a wallpapering table and the back of a Mini Traveller – at Lanchester traction engine rally in August 1974 are Mike Henderson (yellow jumper), Andrew Scott (in red shirt) and the then Treasurer, John Richardson, in suit and tie! *John Hunt*

THE NORTH EASTERN LOCOMOTIVE PRESERVATION GROUP
IN CONJUNCTION WITH THE BRITISH STAFF ASSOCIATION SOUTH BLYTH

ask you to a

CLUB
NIGHT

in the RAILWAY CLUB
Edward Street, Blyth

on *Friday*, 10th March, 1967
from 8 p.m — 12 midnight

Music for dancing supplied by the fabulous

"STOKERS"

EXTENDED LICENCE
GAMES WITH FABULOUS PRIZES
ADMISSION ONLY 2s 6d. [advance tickets on sale]

all proceeds go to help save a J27 steam locomotive

NORTH EASTERN LOCOMOTIVE PRESERVATION GROUP
&
B.1. PRESERVATION SOCIETY
Present
SYMPHONY IN
STEAM

At the ODEON CINEMA CHINGFORD MOUNT E.4. on SATURDAY *evening* 9th DECEMBER 1967 IN AID OF THE PRESERVATION OF L.N.E.R. LOCOS CLASS B1.J27. Q6. THE PROGRAMME FEATURES 9 FILMS INCLUDING:- FLYING FOX 1926 OH Mr. PORTER AND FLYING SCOTSMAN 1929 30 mins INTERMISSION FOR REFRESHMENTS A DISPLAY OF LOCOMOTIVE NAME PLATES AND OTHER RAILWAY ITEMS INCLUDING MODEL STEAM LOCOS CAN BE VIEWED. LOCO DRAWINGS & PHOTO'S ETC., ON SALE PRICE OF ADMISSION: CIRCLE 10/6 STALLS 7/6 ALL SEATS BOOKABLE DOORS OPEN 11 P.M. FILMS COMMENCE 11-30 P.M. APPLICATION FOR TICKETS TO: A.G. Priestley, 16. St Johns Rd. Chingford E.4. OR TO THE Manager, Odeon Cinema, Chingford Mount. E.4. ENCLOSING S.A.E.
ALL CHEQUES & POSTAL ORDERS PAYABLE TO: N.E.L.P.G.

A Club Night at the South Blyth BR Staff Club wasn't too successful. But failures were offset by some unlikely successes. An evening of films in far-off Chingford, Essex, in conjunction with attempts to save a 'B1' for preservation was a great hit. Such was the unbridled enthusiasm at the time that no sensible fund-raising idea was rejected!

On 9 September 1967 the sun finally set on BR steam in the North East. Symbolically, a 'J27' crosses Bebside Viaduct in south-east Northumberland. *Gerry Dixon*

At one of the first working parties on 1 December 1967, after the purchase of No 65894, Eric Maxwell, Cliff Cox and Peter Proud apply red oxide paint to the boiler of the 'J27' at Tyne Dock. *Maurice Burns*

5 THE FIRST RESTORATION OF THE 'J27' AND 'Q6' TO WORKING ORDER

Over the 50 years of the NELPG's history there have been many locomotive overhauls, but the first restorations were special, as enthusiasts from all walks of life but with no previous experience on steam locomotives looked for the first time at how to restore one. There was a pioneering spirit in those early days and some brave decisions were made that could, in the past, never be reported.

new cab roof from No 65882 was acquired, as was boiler cleating from No 65879 and an ex-NER dome from No 65811. The biggest change, however, involved a secret move of No 65894 from Tyne Dock, diesel-hauled, to Thomsons scrapyard in Stockton-on-Tees, in order for its tender to be exchanged with that of No 65882, which was in better condition. The NELPG never received a bill!

Volunteers aged between 15 and 23 pose for the camera whilst preparing the 'Q6' for its first hydraulic test at Thornaby Roundhouse in July 1969. Volunteers shown include Andrew Teesdale, Peter Hutchinson, Maurice Burns, Dave Eadington, Len Mayhew, Angela Plane and John Hardy. *John Boyes/Armstrong Trust*

As NELPG members struggled to save the 'Q6' in late 1967, work progressed steadily on the 'J27' at Tyne Dock. A host of spares was accumulated from scrapyards, including engine springs and vacuum brake equipment, and no less than 5 tons of firebricks from North Blyth thanks to a tip-off from Ian Storey. Items from other withdrawn 'J27s' were exchanged at Tyne Dock, with Peter Proud taking a prominent role. A

Cleaning boiler tubes and repainting at Tyne Dock was good training for raw volunteers and, we thought, a major achievement at the time, but the more difficult task of restoring the engine mechanically was beyond volunteers' expertise. In early 1968 approaches were therefore made to the National Coal Board (NCB), which was still repairing its own steam locomotives at Philadelphia. A negotiation with

A late Sunday working party at Tyne Dock in 1967. Among the volunteers on view are Peter Woodhouse, Neville Stead, Eric Maxwell, Peter Proud and Cliff Cox. *Maurice Burns*

the NCB was successful, and on 29 March 1968 No 65894 was towed from Tyne Dock to Philadelphia for examination and repair.

Inevitably, work on No 65894 was to be an expensive business so in July 1968 the J27 Restoration Fund was launched and, over the next nine months, raised in excess of £800. In October the engine

successfully passed a hydraulic test, in the presence of an Insurance Inspector, then, on 15 November, came the engine's memorable first steaming in NELPG ownership. Mechanical work then followed, including repairs to the big-end brasses, re-metalling of the eccentrics, and overhaul of all of the cab fittings. The cost of these repairs totalled £625. On their

The first 'J27' steam test at Philadelphia on 15 November 1968 with Lambton No 5 behind. *John Hunt*

No 63395 stands inside the otherwise deserted roundhouse at West Hartlepool in December 1968. *Maurice Burns*

completion, the 'J27' was then specially steamed for members at Philadelphia on 15 February 1969, an event that coincided with the end of steam operation on the NCB's extensive system around Philadelphia, and the demise of the Lambton tanks.

Meanwhile, following the saving of the 'Q6' on 1 April 1968, thoughts turned to its restoration.

However, the former wagon works at Tyne Dock, where the engine was housed, was structurally unsound, so in early October No 63395 was diesel-hauled from Tyne Dock to West Hartlepool.

During the four months the engine stayed in the Hartlepool roundhouse, members worked in poor conditions to prepare the locomotive for hydraulic

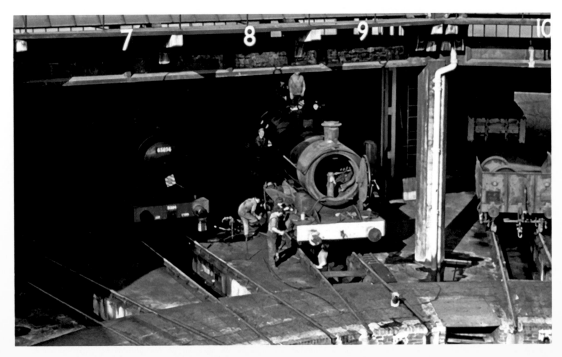

The view of a working party inside Thornaby roundhouse in December 1969, with the 'J27' on No 8 road and the 'Q6' on No 9 road. *Maurice Burns*

testing and repainting. On one particular occasion it appeared that the snow was deeper inside the roundhouse than it was outside! Reputedly staff with a sense of humour put No 63395 on the loco roster board one day, then watched the driver find out that there *really* was a 'Q6' on shed! It was not surprising that, for the second time, the engine's home was declared unsafe, and on 17 February 1969 No 63395 was moved to Thornaby.

Thornaby's roundhouse and workshop was built by BR in 1958 as the last new steam loco depot. Conditions there were far better than any of our locomotive's previous homes. Back at Philadelphia, the NCB could not do the required repairs to the axle boxes and, after discussions with local BR managers, it was established that Thornaby could offer the necessary skills, and a locomotive wheel drop for easy removal of the axle boxes.

While No 65894 was now capable of being steamed for the move from Philadelphia to Thornaby, there was in place a ban on the movement of any steam locomotive over BR metals, so officially No 65894 should have been diesel-hauled. However, John Bellwood clearly fancied a steam footplate ride and authorised the 'J27' to break the steam ban and move in steam to Thornaby. We shall never know if high office had a word afterwards! The sound of a 'J27' on BR metals was therefore heard again on 11 April 1969, when No 65894 made a very public statement

by going through Newcastle Central station in order to turn, in the middle of the national steam ban! It also returned to one of its old stamping grounds, the coast line through Sunderland and Hartlepool to Thornaby, catching up a Newcastle-York parcels express in the process. As No 65894 steamed southwards with John Bellwood in the cab, passengers on station platforms gazed in astonishment!

The move of both engines to Thornaby saw the start of a long association with the staff at that shed. It was less convenient for Tyneside volunteers and some, particularly those with an interest in industrial steam, focused their future efforts on the infant Tanfield Railway. However, because of the good facilities Thornaby provided, such as covered accommodation, loco inspection pits, compressed air, oxygen cutting equipment, overhead crane, washing facilities and a friendly storeman, new volunteers joined the group. The Group was very fortunate that two members, Peter Hutchinson and Maurice Burns, both then aged 22, had just finished their engineering apprenticeships and were confident in both the engineering challenge ahead and the organising of regular working parties. Volunteers such as Terry Newman, Nick Carter, John Hardy, Geoff Scurr, David Eadington, Andrew Teasdale, Dave Hancock, Alan Higgitt, Jeff Brand and Chris Cubitt joined the team, with an age range from just 16 to 23.

We soon got to know some of the Thornaby shed staff, starting at the top with the shed master,

After the fracture repair on the front tubeplate, a superheater element is refitted to the 'Q6' in the Thornaby roundhouse by Chris Cubitt, Dave Eadington, Jeff Brand, John Boyes (RAF), Geoff Scurr and Maurice Burns.
Maurice Burns

NELPG members load five tons of free firebricks into Ian Storey's trailer at North Blyth shed in 1968. In the picture are Ian Storey, Peter W. Robinson and Chris Lawson. *Maurice Burns*

Mr Windlass, and his deputy Phil Crosby. They were sympathetic to our cause, as was Jimmy Dean, the mechanical foreman, and Bob Willis, the maintenance supervisor, but we did occasionally get into trouble – more of that later. There was no safety briefing and no signing-in procedure – volunteers would just walk into the roundhouse as if we owned it. Such happy times – we could not believe it!

The main task was the 'Q6' boiler hydraulic test, and straight away the shed's last boilersmith, Joe Glass, offered advice. Our first ever NELPG volunteer hydraulic boiler test was on No 63395, and it was an absolute shock when we discovered water leaking out of a fracture in the front tube plate hidden behind the superheater header. What happened could not be told at the time, but the implications of this were so serious – had we preserved the right engine? When we selected a 'Q6' to preserve we knew that No 63395 had been one of the last through Darlington Works in 1965, and we had the BR boiler records that showed it to be generally good for a high-mileage engine. But we did not have anyone with experience to do a 'cold' or 'in steam' exam that today, looking back, should have been done. If we had known about the fracture, No

63395 would certainly not have been preserved.

The seriousness of the situation was brought home to the Committee when the NELPG boiler insurance company would not allow a weld repair of the fracture. They insisted on a front tube plate replacement, which, in 1969, no one in steam preservation had ever done. In desperation, Maurice made a special trip to the insurance company head office in Manchester in an attempt to change its mind – and failed. The Group now had a half-restored locomotive that it could not now afford to complete and looked destined to remain a static museum exhibit.

The Group was still convinced that a weld repair was safe, and Maurice consulted pressure vessel and welding engineers at his employers, Davy International. They agreed that it was a safe repair and now there was only one course of action – to change insurance companies. A boiler inspector from an alternative insurance company, who lived locally, was approached and, over tea at his home, approved the weld procedure. The relief that someone would allow a repair was immense, and our policy with the previous company was cancelled. These were brave and monumental decisions for such young volunteers.

In the pursuit of spares, John Hardy, Peter Hutchinson and Peter W. Robinson remove parts of a vacuum ejector for fitting to the 'Q6' and the Lambton tanks from an LMS 2-6-0 at Arnott Young's Dinsdale scrapyard in April 1968.
Maurice Burns

With the fracture now fixed, enthusiasm was sky high and, under the leadership of Joe Glass, members were shown how to remove and fit boiler tubes. Working parties were on Saturdays and it became a tradition that one of us would go out to Thornaby and get fish and chips and bottles of Newcastle Brown Ale. We consumed them sitting on the edge of the turntable pit – we never thought about the implications of drinking beer in a BR loco shed, and nothing was ever said!

After a while we knew everyone at Thornaby and we could, unofficially, help ourselves to anything – but this enthusiasm got volunteers into trouble! The 'Q6' tender platework behind the cab lockers was badly holed. Lying around were lots of large sheets of steel plate, some more than 10 feet long – just the job! Ian Storey did a superb of job cutting the long curve for the top of the plate, which looked like a D shape. When fitted it looked great. However, the next day at work Maurice Burns had a phone call from the shed master: 'Can you pop in and see me at lunchtime please?' So off he went, not sure what he wanted to talk about. In his office that overlooked the shed yards, the shed master said he had spotted that, on a large sheet of plate near the stores, a huge long sweeping D-shaped curve had been carefully cut out and it looked like nothing from a diesel. 'Next time, Maurice, remember to cut it square,

then no one would ever notice the plate was missing.' That was so typical of the spirit of Thornaby staff – they were on our side.

By 5 September 1969 No 63395 had passed its hydraulic test, but by this time funds were running low, so the occasion was used to launch the Q6 Restoration Appeal. Volunteers fitted a brick arch in the firebox for the first time, using those proper firebricks (not concrete as today) that the Group had acquired from North Blyth shed in 1968.

Although an offer had been received from the newly opened Keighley & Worth Valley Railway, the Group decided at an early stage that the prospective North Yorkshire Moors Railway would provide a suitable home, with its challenging gradients, potential length, and proximity to Teesside. Vacuum brake fitting was necessary for working on the NYMR, but the Group had a problem. There were no LNER-style ejectors, and only the LMS pattern was available from scrapyards. The LMS ejectors were frequently fixed to the smokebox, which would have done nothing for the graceful lines of the 'Q6'. People felt strongly about such matters, but we dismantled and bought an LMS brake system from an Ivatt 2-6-0 at Arnott Young scrapyard in Dinsdale, near Darlington.

We did not follow the normal layout but fitted the ejector under the cab floor with exhaust steam going to the tender water tank. This became known as the 'MSB patented steam condensing "Q6"'! It did work faultlessly, even if exhaust steam was seen emerging from the tender water tank if the filler cap was left off, and early pictures of the 'Q6' show it hauling passenger trains with no ejector exhaust pipe along the boiler.

As the first steaming drew near, there was a problem. The BR steam ban was still in place throughout the UK, so would we be able to steam the 'Q6'? Yes, of course, but in secret! On 18 October 1969, No 63395, just two years since withdrawal from BR service, was lit up by NELPG volunteers. It was a special moment, as this was the first time we had been totally responsible. As the highly polished engine with burnished motion and handrails moved from the roundhouse to the turntable, all was well. No real problems at all. The engine was moved to a line to the east of the loco shed where every volunteer was given a go on the regulator, and well deserved it was too.

At this time, the tender of the 'Q6' was host to an ever increasing collection of spares and tools. The problem of storage of such items was becoming acute, especially as completion of the 'Q6' was imminent. So, in February 1970 the Group solved the problem in the best practical way, by purchasing a 10-ton-capacity van, DE 539329. Built in 1923 to a Great Central design and fitted with a vacuum brake and electric light, it was truly a bargain at £90, particularly when the original

asking price was £166. Even better, it was located in the sidings just at the back of Thornaby shed, so no transport costs either!

While all this work was under way, the two Lambton tanks – Nos 5 and 29 – had been bought privately by NELPG and NYMR members, and 15 months after the end of steam operations at Philadelphia, No 29 was moved to Thornaby. With three steam locomotives on shed it was beginning to look like the good old days!

Before repainting in NER freight livery (which had been decided by members in a livery ballot) could be carried out, however, No 63395 was moved to Grosmont in response to an urgent request from the NYMR in 1970 for larger locomotives to work special trains at its increasingly popular weekend steam galas. Following a satisfactory steam test, No 63395 was towed in steam, together with Lambton tank No 29, by a diesel from Thornaby to Grosmont on 25 June. The first 'Q6' ever to haul a passenger train left Grosmont station at 12.15 on Saturday the 27th. Resplendent in BR livery, it successfully tackled the long 1 in 49 gradient to Goathland for the first time, and all marvelled at a sight that had previously just been a dream!

The 'Q6' was to be the mainstay of the NYMR motive power, together with the Lambton 0-6-2Ts Nos 5 and 29, until the arrival of the 'J27', restored as an

It is June 1970, the 'Q6' restoration is complete and the team pose for the camera. Top: Jeff Brand, Peter Hutchinson, Alan Higgitt and Maurice Burns. Bottom: Terry Newman, Dave Eadington, Chris Cubitt, Stan Hindmarch, Dave Hancock and Mick Dewing. *Maurice Burns*

No 63395 stands outside the Thornaby roundhouse after its first steaming, in the condition it would have come out of Darlington Works in the 1960s, with a three-link coupling and steam brake. *Maurice Burns*

The first large steam locomotives to reach the infant NYMR arrived by rail; here Nos 29 and 63395, both in steam but hauled by a diesel, approach Lealholm on 25 June 1970. *John Hunt*

No 63395 takes its first passenger train up the 1 in 49 at Water Ark on 27 June 1970. *John Hunt*

The 'Q6', in interim LNER livery, heads a train, including a Hull & Barnsley Railway coach, at Darnholm in 1971; note the absence of a vacuum exhaust pipe running along the boiler with just the vacuum bag visible under the nearside buffer. *Maurice Burns*

With the ICI loco depot in the background, a resplendent No 2392 stands in steam
at Billingham on 16 October 1971 with the Group's first stores van behind it. *John Hunt*

NER 'P3', in October 1971. In August 1970, however, the number and livery of the 'Q6' were changed to LNER No 3395, with the judicious use of 'Fablon' numbers and letters. This was rumoured to be the result of concern from BR that it did not want its new modern image damaged by the sight of steam engines still operating in BR livery.

At the same time as No 63395 was being moved to Grosmont, a lightning decision by BR finally resulted in No 65894 being moved onto the wheel drops at Thornaby, so that the axle boxes could be repaired. With the delivery of No 63395 to the NYMR, work could now be concentrated on No 65894, so repairs and restoration recommenced in earnest.

On the completion of the mechanical repairs, however, including the fitting of LNER-pattern vacuum brake gear, there was now no good reason for the locomotive to stay at Thornaby, and the threat of having to pay rent meant that a search was on for an alternative home to complete its restoration.

Fortunately, ICI kindly offered the engine a home at its works at Billingham, and the 'J27' was moved there on 5 January 1971 for fitting of steam heating gear and repainting into NER freight livery of black lined out in red as 'P3' No 2392. With no deadline to meet, great care was taken to achieve as good a finish as possible, and the superb restoration was completed in October 1971 at a cost of more than £1,000.

The 'P3' was steamed at Billingham on 16 October 1971 and, when given the freedom of the ICI East Grid Sidings, No 2392 stirred the memories by toying with a 600-ton coal train. A week later the 'P3' was en route to Grosmont, and a new lease of life.

On Monday 25 October 1971 the official handing over of No 2392 on loan to the NYMR took place. Representatives of BR, ICI and the press looked on as Richard Rowntree, then NYMR Chairman, performed the ceremony with the Group's Chairman, Ian Storey, which culminated in the ceremonial affixing of the distinctive NER-type brass number plates to the

Above and below: No 2392 shunts a lengthy rake of old NER wagons on Billingham's East Grid sidings on the same day. *John Hunt*

cab side of the 'P3'. These celebrations had added significance because they marked, almost to the day, the fifth anniversary of the founding of the NELPG. In those five years, the Group's initial aims had been realised, more than £8,000 had been raised, and the Group possessed two fine working examples of North Eastern Railway motive power.

The NYMR started its first public passenger services on Easter Sunday 25 April 1973 and NELPG members were proud that the Group's 'P3' No 2392 was the steam motive power, and equally proud that three NELPG volunteers who had worked so hard on the 'P3' and 'Q6' restorations were on duty – driver Chris Cubitt, fireman Maurice Burns and guard Nick Carter.

Another highlight occurred on 1 May 1973 when the 'P3', in its 50th year, piloted No 29 on the North Yorkshire Moors Railway re-opening special, carrying the Duchess of Kent from Grosmont to Pickering.

The 1969 to 1971 overhauls were nothing compared to the restoration work undertaken 50 years later but, because they were done by such very young volunteers, it was a major technical achievement, safely carried out. We were so proud of what we had done, and many volunteers 50 years on can remember sitting in the warm cab of No 63395 at the end of its first steaming, not wanting to go home. The resultant publicity put the NELPG in the spotlight and it has never looked back.

The NELPG Committee of (left to right) Maurice Burns, Chris Lawson, Chris Cubitt, Major Bryce Greenfield, Richard Wheeler, Peter Hutchinson, John Hunt, John Richardson, Ian Storey and Cliff Cox pose in front of the 'P3' at Grosmont on 25 October 1971. *John Hunt*

6 'KI' No 62005 IS DONATED TO THE NELPG

The official North British works photograph of the final 'KI', No 62070.

In the last years of steam in the North East, a number of relatively modern locomotives of the 'KI' Class were transferred to local depots to replace ailing 'J27s'. But when the last 'KIs' were withdrawn, there was no individual who wanted to buy one, or a preservation society set up to raise funds, as NELPG had done to save the 'J27' and 'Q6'.

The survival of a representative of the 'KI' Class into preservation is yet another remarkable story, where luck played a significant part. It was saved, without fanfare or enthusiasts really being aware of what was going on, by some very quick-thinking individuals who all had a strong affection for steam and the NYMR.

No 62005 was one of 70 Class 'KI' mixed-traffic 2-6-0s designed by A. H. Peppercorn as a development of Class 'KI/I'. They were built by the North British Locomotive Company, Glasgow, in 1949 and 1950. 'KIs' saw wide service in the Scottish, Eastern and North

Eastern Regions of British Railways, from Mallaig in the north to March in the south, although No 62005 spent all of its life based in the North East.

Following completion on 10 June 1949, the engine was run in from Glasgow Eastfield depot, before moving to Heaton. Spells were thereafter spent at Darlington, Leeds (Ardsley) and York. It was while allocated to York, and following its last overhaul in Darlington North Road Works in early 1965, that it was chosen to partner the privately preserved Class 'K4' No 3442 *The Great Marquess* on the 'Whitby Moors Rail Tour' on 6 March 1965. This was the last BR steam train to work between Scarborough and Whitby, and between Whitby and Pickering, Malton and York. In early 1966 a motive power crisis in the Blyth area resulted in No 62005 being transferred to North Blyth, to assist the ageing and run-down 'J27s' in coping with that depot's mineral traffic.

By January 1967 46 'KIs' had been scrapped, but

'K1' 62005 at Castleton Sidings, between Rochdale and Castleton stations, on Saturday 18 July 1959, with an empty stock working from Halifax to Lightbowne Sidings, Newton Heath, after working a returning holiday extra to Halifax. *Richard Greenwood*

24 were still hard at work. York still had three, North Blyth eight, Tyne Dock seven, Sunderland one and Hartlepool five. Many of these engines had not seen a locomotive works for years and had amassed nearly 70,000 miles without any sort of overhaul. The 'K1' big-end knock was renowned, but it never affected the engines' performance.

The Royal Train was in regular use in the 1960s and, with steam virtually eliminated, it was usually diesel-hauled. Steam heating could be provided by a diesel, but only by keeping its engine running – not necessarily conducive to a good night's sleep for the train's occupants. With only a few months remaining for steam in the area, the Queen's visit to the North East on 22 March 1967, which involved an overnight stay, was just such an opportunity. The annual distribution of the Royal Maundy Money by Her Majesty took place in Durham Cathedral, prior to which the Royal Train was stabled overnight on the Ponteland branch. It was decided, no doubt with a little influence by John Bellwood, to replace the

incoming diesel at Gosforth by a steam locomotive, which would haul the train to its stabling point and continue to provide heating. For this working, No 62005 was moved from North Blyth to Heaton shed and especially prepared for this Royal duty, including the fitting of a 52B Heaton shed plate.

No 62005 was also the natural choice for the Stephenson Locomotive Society's 'Three Dales Railtour' on 20 May 1967. This 195-mile railtour, with a six-coach train, started at Stockton-on-Tees and ran to Northallerton, then via Bedale to Redmire in Wensleydale, on to the Richmond and Catterick Camp branches in Swaledale, and finally to Stanhope and Westgate in Weardale, before returning to Middlesbrough.

As the run-down of steam continued in the North East, York withdrew its last 'K1' in April 1967, Sunderland followed on 17 May, and Hartlepool finished its last three 'K1s' on 1 July, but Tyne Dock kept its last examples in traffic until the end of North East steam on 9 September. The survivors at this

No 62005 at Prospect Hill Junction, Whitby, with the 'Whitby Moors' railtour on 6 March 1965. The 'K1' is drawing the train forward towards Whitby West Cliff station, so that the 'K4', seen behind the train, can couple onto the back to take the train down to Whitby Town on the right-hand of the two tracks. The tour had originated at Manchester Victoria and No 3442 *The Great Marquess* took over from 'Jubilee' No 45698 *Mars* at Wakefield Kirkgate. The 'K1' joined the 'K4' at Market Weighton for the onward journey to Filey, Scarborough, Whitby, Malton and York, where the 'K1' was detached. The 'K4' then continued to Wakefield where No 45698 once again took over. *John Boyes*

No 62005 passes the Stanhope up distant signal en route from Bishop Auckland to Westgate with the SLS 'Three Dales' railtour on 20 May 1967. *Phil Waterfield*

date were Nos 62005, 62007, 62011 (an ex-Fort William engine), 62045 (which had been overhauled in Cowlairs Works, Glasgow, after North Road had shut) and 62050. The last day of steam in the North East coincided with a main-line railtour by GWR 'Castle' Class No 7029 *Clun Castle* to Newcastle Central station. Previous gauging trials found that *Clun Castle*'s cylinders fouled the platforms, so No 62005 was selected to take over the train at King Edward Bridge for the short journey into Newcastle. For this duty, the BR engine cleaners did a great job, including painting the chimney top of the 'K1' with gold paint to outshine the 'Castle', which of course it did!

Following this 'Indian Summer' of high-profile activity, the 'K1' was transferred to Holbeck depot, Leeds, later in September, but it was back at Thornaby before the end of the year and nominally withdrawn from service on 31 December 1967. However, on Boxing Day of that year No 62005 was hauled to North Tees Sidings and spent the early part of 1968 as a stationary boiler, supplying steam to the Phillips Oil Refinery. The locomotive was manned by Hartlepool firemen who did not particularly relish the job after having been accustomed to riding on Class 37 diesel locomotives. As the locomotive was not standing on a pit, difficulty was experienced in disposing of the firebox ash. This resulted in burnt rocker bars and the distortion of the ash pan. On completion of these duties, No 62005 was towed back to Leeds Neville Hill shed, where it awaited an uncertain future.

No 62005 seemed likely to be scrapped, as no individual or society had been formed to preserve it. However, the privately preserved Class 'K4' No

3442 *The Great Marquess*, owned by the Rt Hon Lord Garnock, had a problem with its firebox. It is believed that John Bellwood is likely to have suggested to Lord Garnock to take an option to purchase No 62005, with a view to exchanging boilers with the 'K4', hence the former's move to Neville Hill shed to be with the 'K4'. Such thinking was necessary, at the time, as all steam workshops had closed and steam overhaul skills in the preservation movement, especially on major boiler work, were very limited. John Bellwood had already allowed time to pass in order to find someone to buy a 'J72' from Blyth, had played a part in keeping the 'J27' and 'Q6' at Tyne Dock and, with an eye on the growing developments on the infant North Yorkshire Moors Railway, he may just have suggested the boiler swap in order to stop the 'K1' being quickly scrapped. Fortunately the option to purchase the locomotive from BR was taken up by Lord Garnock, Geoffrey Drury, George Nissen and Brian Hollingsworth, without the world at large being aware of it.

The 'K1' was not in working order, and sat alongside the then unrestored 'N7' and the 'K4' with its boiler problems. In the event, the work involved in changing over the boilers looked like being too costly and, moreover, there seemed a fair possibility, later realised, that modern welding techniques could effect a repair. That left a decision to be made about what to do with No 62005.

The first anyone in NELPG knew about this quandary was in February 1972 when, without any warning, a letter came through the letterbox of the Secretary, Chris Lawson, to the effect that No 62005 was to be offered to NELPG as an outright gift. By

No 62005, complete with fireman, provides steam for the Phillips refinery. *John Boyes/Armstrong Trust*

Following its private purchase, No 62005 stands inside Neville Hill depot at Leeds in April 1972 flanked by 'K4' No 3442 *The Great Marquess* and 'N7' No 69621. *Maurice Burns*

1972, of course, the NYMR was planning its reopening and many were aware of the suitability of the 'K1' to meet the NYMR's long-term need for additional steam power. NELPG members and its Committee had done the virtually impossible in saving a 'J27' and a 'Q6' the hard way! Now, four years on, they were being offered another North East locomotive without doing anything. It was unbelievable.

The NELPG was well known to the four owners of No 62005, because of its achievements with the 'J27' and the 'Q6', and it was considered by them that the Group was best placed to tackle No 62005's restoration. It was also considered that the additional incentive provided by making over the locomotive as an outright gift, together with the simplicity of such an arrangement, would outweigh any possible advantages in retaining direct control of its destiny. This was duly done using Brian Hollingsworth's No 45428 Stanier Class Five Locomotive Society Ltd as a convenient instrument. It is likely that it was Brian who suggested that the 'K1' be donated to NELPG, being on the BR Board with responsibility for civil engineering. With great excitement, he had related the tale that when

the new Thornaby shed was being planned in the 1950s it was his personal idea that there *had* to be a roundhouse! What gave him the greatest of pleasure was that Thornaby had already been used by NELPG volunteers as a restoration base, and now the 'K1' was to be restored in his roundhouse – as he referred to it!

Many NELPG members had a soft spot for 'K1s' – a regular sight across the North East – and some had even cleaned No 62005 at Hartlepool shed before the 'Three Dales' railtour in 1967. With volunteers keen to tackle the 'K1' restoration at Thornaby, the formal decision to accept the engine as a donation to the NELPG was taken by the membership at an EGM on 19 May 1972. A K1 Appeal Fund was immediately launched, in an attempt to raise an overhaul cost of £1,500, the bulk of this cost being for a set of small tubes and axle box repairs.

The engine was towed by a diesel from Neville Hill to Thornaby and placed in the roundhouse. This move could have been another heavy unwanted cost to the NELPG, but John Bellwood had an alternative plan. He organised, in conjunction with the Thornaby shed

At the well-attended Thornaby depot open day on 10 September 1972, note the public access to the footplate of the 'J new coal wagons built at Shildon, a 'Deltic' diesel and, of course, the 'K1', recently arrived from Leeds. Note, too, the NE sales stall by the 'J27' with Peter Woodhouse and John Hunt busy selling photographs for the 'fund' and Val Burns in the explaining the controls. *Maurice Burns*

master, for Thornaby to have an 'Open Day' that would remarkably coincide with the 'K1' move, and that locomotive would be used to demonstrate the wheel drop facility. The transfer move from Leeds, on 14 June 1972, was therefore free!

Following the open day on 10 September (which also featured the NELPG's 'P3' and 'A4' 'Pacific' No 4498 *Sir Nigel Gresley*), the restoration work started in earnest, with the aim of bringing the engine back into service in LNER apple green livery, lined out in black and white, as requested by the former owners. The restoration work was considerable, with the total renewal of all 141 2-inch tubes by members, who had earlier learned re-tubing skills on the 'Q6' in 1969.

Ashpan platework repairs, a new pattern for a set of replacement firebars, axle box liners and piston and valve rings were some of the other work required.

Throughout 1973, and into early 1974, restoration proceeded slowly, on weekday evenings, until the finish was in sight. After the burning of much midnight oil, Sunday 19 May 1974 saw the culmination of almost two years of work on the 'K1', when it was successfully steamed – for the first time in preservation. This took place in Thornaby roundhouse, just as Brian Hollingsworth would have wanted! The event brought back happy memories of the first steam test of the 'Q6' in the same roundhouse, four and a half years previously. As the engine emerged from the depths of

Unlike the 'J27' and 'Q6', much of the restoration of the 'K1' took place in the Thornaby repair shed. The 2-6-0 is seen here on the wheel drops for axlebox repairs, alongside a Class 37 diesel, in 1973. *John Hunt*

The overhaul complete, No 2005 makes its first movement on the Thornaby roundhouse turntable on 6 June 1974 in the capable hands of driver Stan Hindmarch. *John Hunt*

With BR driver Stan Hindmarch in the cab, NELPG volunteers pose for the camera in May 1974 at Thornaby on the occasion of the first steaming of the 'K1'. From the top, left to right, are included Maurice Burns, John Whitbread, Nick Carter, Andy Teasdale, Alan Higgitt, Danny Fawcett, Terry Newman, Phil Jay, Dave Holroyde, George Hawxwell, Ian Storey, Ian Pearson, Paul Smith, Dave Hancock and Len Mayhew. *Maurice Burns*

the roundhouse, now decked in apple green as LNER No 2005, its splendour could be fully appreciated. The £1,500 raised by members for the K1 Appeal had been money well spent.

Ten days later, No 2005 ran under its own steam from Thornaby to Grosmont, then took a test train up the 1 in 49 gradient to Goathland. On Saturday 8 June it officially entered service on the NYMR by hauling the 10.50am train from Grosmont to Goathland. Prior to departure, a short handing-over ceremony was held at Grosmont station. Speeches were made by the then NELPG Chairman, Ian Storey, and by the Chairman of what had now become the North Yorkshire Moors Historical Railway Trust, Richard Rowntree, who expressed his admiration at the results of the work done on the locomotive by Group members. The

'K1'-hauled train included Brian Hollingsworth's GWR saloon, where the NYMR President, Lord Downe, hosted lunch for the former owners, the restoration team and their partners, with refreshments served by Lord Downe's butler.

At the celebrations for the first restoration of the 'K1', no one could have foreseen how the engine's history would unfold over the next 40 years. One thing is for sure, though. Those who saved No 62005 from being scrapped, namely Lord Garnock, Geoffrey Drury, George Nissen and Brian Hollingsworth, would be very pleased with the decision they made all those years ago. Certainly the NELPG cannot thank them enough for their generosity and will be forever in their debt.

7 The Lambton tanks

The NELPG also had an early involvement with Lambton 0-6-2 tanks Nos 5 and 29. No 5 had been built by Robert Stephenson and Co Ltd at Darlington in 1909, and No 29 by Kitson & Co Ltd at Leeds in 1904, both for the Lambton Collieries Ltd in County Durham. The engines were unusual in being of 0-6-2 wheel arrangement, rather than the 0-6-0 and 0-4-0 arrangements widely adopted for industrial locomotives. Up to 13 0-6-2Ts were employed over the extensive colliery system between Houghton-le-Spring and Herrington collieries, Lambton coke works and Penshaw sidings, and over the North Eastern Railway's line from there to Pallion, Sunderland and thence to Lambton staiths on the River Wear.

The staiths closed and operation over what was then a British Railways line from Penshaw ceased early in 1966. Together with colliery closures, this rang the death knell for the Lambton tanks. Nos 5 and 29

Official works photographs of Nos 5 and 29.

No 5 pulls empty coal wagons out of Lambton coke works on 15 February 1969,
the final day of steam operation. *Graham Holt*

proved to be the last in service, being withdrawn when the system was dieselised. Their final workings were on 15 February 1969, when a heavy overnight snowfall blanketed the system. The day dawned with the sun rising into an azure sky. It was a memorable finale. Both engines lay in store for 15 months before being purchased, No 5 by NELPG members Bob and Sylvia

Jones of Derby, and No 29 by the Lambton No 29 Syndicate, a group of NELPG and NYMR members.

Both locomotives had received general overhauls at Philadelphia in July 1968 and were therefore in good order. With minimum attention, No 29 moved to Thornaby for vacuum brake fitting by NELPG members, before accompanying No 63395 to

No 29 rounds the curve at Philadelphia with coal from Houghton colliery, also on 15 February 1969. *John Hunt*

Grosmont on 25 June 1970. No 5 was less fortunate, since some fittings and copper pipework were missing and required replacement. The brake system also needed attention before the engine could be moved to Thornaby for vacuum brake fitting and a quick repaint. Considerable work was ultimately needed to put No 5 back into full working order, and volunteers spent long hours at Philadelphia and Thornaby before the engine was delivered to the NYMR on 28 August 1970. Both locomotives subsequently gave sterling service and proved very popular with crews and management alike, until replaced by larger locomotives more suitable for hauling the NYMR's ever bigger trains.

On the NYMR, No 5 heads an early morning four-coach train at Esk Valley in May 1988. *John Hunt*

No 29 heads up the 1 in 49 at Water Ark with a Grosmont-Goathland train in the spring of 1977. *Roger Bastin*

8 THE NYMR FROM GROSMONT TO PICKERING

In June 1967, not long after the NELPG's formation, the first meeting was held of the North Yorkshire Moors Railway Preservation Society. Its aim was to preserve the railway from Grosmont, near Whitby, to Ellerbeck, the summit of the line, which originally headed over the moors to Pickering and thence to Malton and York. In November 1968 volunteers were given possession of the route and work could begin on preparing the line for its new role. In July 1970, only three years after that first meeting, the NYMR ran its first passenger trains, albeit for members only, until a Light Railway Order could be obtained. From that very first day of NYMR passenger operations, the NELPG's locomotives have formed an important part of the Railway's motive power. The line's steep gradients and 18-mile length demand more of the locomotive fleet than perhaps any other preserved railway, and the sheer power of the locomotives in the NELPG's collection has been a major asset to the Railway. It was formally reopened from Grosmont through to Pickering on 1 May 1973 and has since gone from strength to strength, eventually extending its services over Network Rail lines from Grosmont to Whitby, and regularly carrying in excess of 300,000 passengers each year.

More recently, as other main-line locos have become available, the pressure on the NELPG to provide power for the NYMR has reduced. This has allowed the Group to pursue opportunities for its engines to work further afield. Nevertheless, the NYMR remains the NELPG's main operating base and, for as long as steam remains supreme, the Group's locomotives will be taking their turn at the NYMR's challenging gradients.

NYMR mileages for NELPG locomotives up until the end of July 2016 were as follows:

65894	60,232
63395	50,580
62005	45,197
69023	4,986

The following pages show locomotives owned by the NELPG at work on the NYMR.

Nos 2392 and 29 climb past Esk Valley with the NYMR's reopening Royal train on 1 May 1973 conveying the Duchess of Kent GCVO and displaying the Royal lamp code. *Maurice Burns*

To mark the fifth anniversary of the Group, the 'P3' and 'Q6' worked passenger and freight trains on 2 November 1971; here the 'P3' leaves Goathland. *Chris Gammell*

No 65894 leaves Goathland on 6 November 1998 with a pick-up goods for Pickering. *John Cooper Smith*

On its inaugural day in NYMR traffic, No 63395 rounds the bend at Darnholm on 27 June 1970. *John Hunt*

The 'Q6', as LNER No 3395, leaves Grosmont with the last train of the day on 31 August 1970. Note the rail-motor on the right and, in the distance, the long-removed Grosmont Junction signal box. *David Idle*

The 'Q6', now as NER 'T2' No 2238, departs from Goathland, with spring snow still lying, in April 1977. Note LMS 'Black Five' No 5428 *Eric Treacy* in the sidings and coaches, including the Barnum brake, on temporary track on the right. *John Hunt*

Having reverted to BR black livery, No 63395 heads a goods train through Northdale on 7 November 2007. *John Hunt*

No 2005 makes light work of the 1 in 49 gradient at Green End on 20 April 1976. *John Whiteley*

No 62005 reflects the low afternoon winter sun at Fen Bog with the breakdown train returning from Pickering to Grosmont on 22 November 1999. *John Whiteley*

No 62005 leaves Levisham northbound on 1 May 2015. *Ken Snowdon*

On 1 May 2013, with the 'J27' under overhaul, it wasn't possible to authentically recreate the Royal reopening train of 1 May 1973. Instead, No 62005 deputised and is seen here with No 29 in charge at Moorgates. *John Hunt*

No 69023 heads a rake of coal hoppers round Kingthorpe curve, near Pickering, in September 1983. *John Hunt*

No 69023 makes light work of the 'Old Gentleman's Saloon' at Water Ark on 19 May 1991. *John Whiteley*

9 S&D 150 CAVALCADE – THE GREATEST DAY FOR STEAM

I975 was a truly momentous year for railway preservationists, since it saw the I50th anniversary of the opening of the Stockton & Darlington Railway, and, as in 1925, appropriate celebrations were planned. However, unlike the 1925 celebrations, which were organised and funded by the LNER, the 1975 celebrations were to be much more complex, being organised by a partnership of local authorities, preservationists and British Rail.

For various reasons, the NELPG story of what really happened all those years ago has never been fully documented because it was thought politic not to do so at the time. With the passing of the years, the full story can now be told, about how the generosity of County Councils, the heartache of failures, errors by inspectors, brave decisions by engineers, exemplary leadership and volunteer team spirit achieved the virtually impossible. What drove volunteers on was the fact that such celebrations don't happen very often. The date was fixed in stone and there would be no second chance. We had to be there, and we were – just! This huge effort led to the NELPG having more locomotives in the Grand Cavalcade than any other volunteer-run society – a truly amazing achievement.

To start at the very beginning, many enthusiasts will have seen the flickering black and white silent film taken in 1925 of the 100th Anniversary Cavalcade of locomotives organised by the LNER. Even though BR had finished with steam in 1968, two County Councils, namely Cleveland and Durham, proud of their rich railway history, wanted to celebrate the 150th anniversary in 1975. This would publicise the area, so, within reason, they would finance it. British Rail was not involved at all initially, but, once the vision was created, backed by good organisation, all of its staff, from top managers to steam engine drivers, came fully on board.

The planning started in the summer of 1972, a whole three years before the event, with an appeal for interested parties to get in touch. The NELPG's Technical Secretary, Maurice Burns, was keen to represent the Group. He not only lived near the route of the Stockton & Darlington Railway, but thought that if the engines that NELPG had preserved could take part in such a piece of railway history, it was an opportunity not to be missed. The whole celebrations were organised by a Joint Committee of County Councils, and interested parties, with Lord Downe as President. There were sub-committees for publicity, events, and the production of an event guidebook. For three years, Maurice served on all four committees, the results of which brought great influence, as the NELPG was the only 'hands-on' society represented that had operational experience of working steam locomotives.

From the very first meeting of the Events Committee, the idea of a week-long exhibition at Shildon wagon works and a Grand Steam Cavalcade from Shildon to Darlington was discussed. The key to it all was the cooperation of the Shildon Works Manager, Geoff Brecknall, and it was Maurice's letter to him of 2 December 1972 that ultimately led to all the events of August 1975.

The NELPG was therefore in the forefront of developments as they happened, and, in the years of planning, made many great friends that, over time, helped the Group enormously. One of these friendships started as a result of Maurice being in the small group that chose which engines should be in the Grand Cavalcade – a task many enthusiasts would dream of. A major problem was that societies would say that their engines would be ready, but they were actually just a heap of parts. The solution was to have an expert carry out a preliminary boiler and mechanical assessment 12 months before the Cavalcade. The person chosen for this task was Bill Harvey, the former Norwich shed master and a true man of steam. As a result, a close friendship developed with Bill that many years later saw him volunteer to help the NELPG and be appointed the Group's President in 1983.

The choice of which locomotives would be invited to take part was a fascinating exercise, and the Group's NER 'P3' and 'Q6' were natural choices to represent the 0-6-0 and 0-8-0 freight locomotives. The Gresley 'K4' No 3442 *The Great Marquess* was the choice to

represent the 2-6-0 mixed-traffic engines but, when it was found that it could not be repaired in time, the NELPG's then newly overhauled 'K1' deputised.

Another friendship that developed was with Mike Satow, an engineer who offered his services to the Joint Committee to build a full-size working replica of *Locomotion*. He had no drawings to work from and, when measuring the original engine, which was then on a plinth at Darlington Bank Top station, in order to produce new drawings, he declared that it would not work! He loved technical discussions, often at his home, and Mike became a key organiser as the event unfolded, and a great friend of the NELPG.

In late 1973 there was a need for someone to liaise between the locomotive owners and British Rail, in order to coordinate inspections and locomotive movements from all over the UK and report to the Joint Committee. Another case of the right man for the job saw George Hinchcliffe of Flying Scotsman Enterprises appointed to this role. George was a great communicator and a man who got things done. It was through the Group's friendship with George that 'K1' No 2005 (and indeed No 4767) was put on the BR approved list for main-line operations with a view to running S&DR 150 trips on the Esk Valley line in the summer of 1975. This action later opened the door to the whole BR network.

In early 1974 the Events Committee was looking for a significant activity to open the exhibition at Shildon wagon works in August 1975. Totally unconnected with this was the fact that the NYMR, which had recently opened, was trying to increase its fleet of larger locomotives in order to operate its services. Brian Hollingsworth's LMS Class 5 4-6-0

No 5428 *Eric Treacy* and Bill Smith's GNR 0-6-0ST No 1247 had already been moved, with help from NELPG members, from Tyseley, Birmingham, to the NYMR. Another of Brian's engines was LMS Class 5 No 44767, which, uniquely, had Stephenson's link motion and was then stored at Carnforth (see Chapter 10).

Maurice came up with the idea of naming No 44767 *George Stephenson* at the opening event, to commemorate the engineer of the Stockton & Darlington Railway. Brian Hollingsworth was enthusiastic about the plan but was concerned about movement costs. The NELPG Committee was then approached to see if its volunteers would be interested in tackling the restoration of No 44767 at Thornaby. The work would have to be done within 12 months and against an end date that could not be put back, as the Cavalcade was now fixed for 31 August 1975. The Committee agreed to take it on – a very high-risk decision considering that three other NELPG engines had been invited to the Cavalcade and one of them, the 'Q6', needed major boiler repairs at Grosmont. The naming proposal was put to the Joint Committee, which thought it a perfect event, so much so that the County Councils agreed to pay all costs for the movement of No 44767 from Carnforth to Thornaby, then, after the Cavalcade, from Thornaby to Grosmont. In addition, the Councils also agreed to meet all the costs for the brass nameplates and commemorative plaques. Without the County Councils financing the movements of No 44767 to the North East, it would have remained at Carnforth and a totally different history for the locomotive would have followed.

In the summer of 1974 the 'P3' and 'K1' were in NYMR traffic, work on No 44767 was yet to start,

At Carnforth, John Whitbread, Andy Teasdale, Nigel Bill, Peter Robinson, Ian Storey, Paul Smith, John Hunt and Maurice Burns take time off from preparing No 4767 for its move to Thornaby in July 1974. *John Hunt*

No 44767 undergoes its overhaul inside the roundhouse at Thornaby in October 1974 . Note its parts, including the superheater elements and dome cover, in the foreground. *Maurice Burns*

and the 'Q6' had not been steamed for three years. The latter engine alone needed boiler tube renewals, the fitting of an LNER-pattern vacuum brake system, mechanical work and full repainting in North Eastern Railway livery as 'T2' Class No 2238, and it all had to be completed within nine months!

NELPG volunteers prepared No 44767 at Carnforth for movement to Thornaby and, after BR inspection, it was towed there on 14 August 1974. Restoration work took place every Monday and Wednesday evening, with the renewal of all small tubes a priority, and by 27 November – just 12 weeks later – the boiler had passed a hydraulic test. It was at this time that our Technical Secretary received a shock when Brian Hollingsworth indicated that he wished to sell his engine, but concern turned to relief when it was announced that Ian Storey, the NELPG Chairman, intended to purchase it for the sum of £7,000, and maintain the same agreements that included a plate on the locomotive 'Restored by the North Eastern Locomotive Preservation Group 1975'. Other work included the overhaul of all boiler fittings, piston valves and the brake system, and by 15 March 1975 the locomotive had had its first steam test. Despite it being only seven months since its arrival on Teesside, the restoration, and repainting into LMS livery as No 4767, was going to plan.

At Grosmont, however, a series of events unfolded

that was impossible to foresee and that was to test all the NELPG volunteers' determination to the limit. The 'Q6' overhaul in the autumn of 1974 had been going well at the NYMR, which was, at that time, responsible for all costs of the maintenance of the NELPG locomotives. Sixty-three 2-inch tubes and ten flue tubes had wasted tube ends in the firebox. The former were replaced with new tubes, but the BR boiler inspector authorised the descaling of the old 5¼-inch flue tubes and their reuse with new ends, a course of action that would save much-needed NYMR funds. However, after doing all the work in reconditioning the 5¼-inch tubes, under hydraulic test at one and a half times the working pressure, a reconditioned flue tube imploded.

This shocked the working members and, after taking advice, they decided to renew the flue tubes they had just fitted and for the NELPG to fund the work. This doubling up of the effort was a major setback and lost more than two months against the Cavalcade deadline. When the ten new flues had been refitted, a further hydraulic test was done, on 20 April 1975. More bad news then resulted, as one of the untouched flues imploded at 240 psi, wrapping itself round the superheater element.

Within 24 hours an emergency NELPG Committee meeting had authorised the renewal of all the old flue tubes, funded by the Group's sales reserve.

In November 1974, volunteers
Peter Hutchinson, Dave Hancock, Alan
Higgitt and John Whitbread labouri-
ously and carefully remove the first
flue tubes from the 'Q6' at Grosmont
for reconditioning with welded new
ends. *Maurice Burns*

No UK supplier could meet the
urgent delivery we wanted, so the
replacements came from Germany.
They were quickly delivered, on 22
May, but to the Technical Secretary's
front garden in Yarm, which was the
order address, rather than the delivery
address at Grosmont! The collapsed
flue tube was carefully removed
without damage to the element,
and all the remaining renewals were
done, helped by three 'T2 Weeks'
when volunteers took holidays. With
repainting in NER lined livery being
undertaken and managed by Len
Clarke, things were starting to look
up. A successful hydraulic test was
followed by a first steam test on 4
August, just three weeks before the
Shildon event. It now looked like plain
sailing to the deadline, but this proved
to be far from the case.

During the Spring Bank Holiday
weekend, the 'P3', in passenger service
on the NYMR, suffered a broken spring
and, rather than immediately being
stopped for repair, the locomotive
continued in use as the NYMR had no
other engines. This decision resulted in
two hot axle boxes. As with the 'Q6',
the NYMR was responsible for the
repair costs. As there was no crane to
lift the engine to carry out the repairs,
any chance of the 'P3' appearing in the
Cavalcade looked remote, particularly
as the NYMR could not decide if it
could afford the high cost of hiring
in two large road cranes to perform
the task. After a whole month had
been lost, a last-minute go-ahead by

Disaster! The BR boiler inspectors
had approved the reuse of the old
flue tubes but under hydraulic test
to 270 psi in February 1975, a flue
tube imploded. Now wider than the
tube hole it is seen being cut out in
sections. After this shock all flue tubes
were renewed. *Maurice Burns*

the NYMR was given to lift the engine – just 14 days before its planned departure for Shildon.

Re-metalling and bedding in, then a further crane hire, saw the engine re-wheeled just two days before departure to Shildon. The entire motion had to be put up and the NYMR said that it did not have staff to do it. With backs against the wall, NELPG volunteers working beyond midnight managed to refit all loco springs, eccentrics and piston valves, then recouple the engine and tender, all in the space of 5 hours. With exhaustion setting in and time running out to fit the connecting rods, the crossheads were secured and the connecting rods loaded into the tender. The Technical Secretary had a plan. He phoned BR and convinced them that the 'P3', with motion in the tender, could be safely put between the 'K1' and 'T2' for movement to Thornaby. Fortunately, BR agreed.

At 9am on Tuesday 19 August, against countless odds, the three NELPG engines departed from Grosmont. However, the Group's luck quickly ran out, as by Battersby the 'T2' had one hot box and the 'P3' two hot boxes. The problem with the axle boxes on both the NER engines was that, due to lack of funds, they were basically as they had been when running on BR. For those technically minded, the axle box design

does not allow for the under-keep lubrication pads to be renewed or checked for water, unlike on more modern engines. In BR days, pads would be renewed at least during every works visit, usually about two years apart. In 1975, some of the pads on our engines had been in place for 12 years.

Both engines were dragged to Thornaby where the Technical Secretary had a meeting with the shed master, who was determined, as was the NELPG, that the engines should be in the Cavalcade, and formulated a plan. This involved NELPG volunteers doing all motion work and BR staff fitting the axle boxes and springs. Volunteers burning the midnight oil saw the motion removed from both engines. BR staff then took over, and, using the wheel drop, removed the brasses. Thornaby shed still had a coppersmith able to do re-metalling work, so progress was fast. The 'T2' was the first to be fully reassembled and was then towed on Friday 22 August to Northallerton Cross Gates for running in. This non-stop run resulted in another hot box. This was a low point. We had to phone all the volunteers again and ask them to do another midnight shift at Thornaby to remove the 'T2' motion. There was also another serious problem. The coppersmith had left to go on holiday. However, the shed master phoned

After incurring two hot axle boxes, the 'P3' had to be lifted at Grosmont by two hired-in road cranes to remove the wheelsets, then refit them, as pictured here on 5 August 1975. *John Hunt*

him up and asked him to come to work on the Sunday to re-metal the brass, which to his credit he did. The bearing was scraped in during the afternoon, and the wheels refitted by BR fitters in the evening. Volunteers scheduled to be at the Shildon Exhibition were then drafted to Thornaby where, led by Len Clarke, they revarnished the 'P3' tender and boiler and repainted the smokebox. Things were looking up!

In the meantime the 'K1' had departed for Darlington, where a small exhibition of locomotives was held in the bay platforms at Darlington Bank Top (now a car park) in the week before the main event at Shildon.

Monday 25 August was a volunteers' day off, to enable them to see the opening of the week-long Shildon exhibition of locomotives and the naming ceremony of No 4767 as George Stephenson by the Rt Hon William Whitelaw MP, whose father had been Chairman of the LNER. It was a proud day for both the locomotive owner and NELPG Chairman Ian Storey and Technical Secretary Maurice Burns, who took part in the ceremony, as well as for all the NELPG volunteers who had restored the engine in less than 12 months. Also on the platform at the naming ceremony

were artist John Wigston, who presented a painting to Mr Whitelaw, and Captain Peter Manisty, Chairman of the ARPS, who had done so much to help save both the 'P3' and the 'T2'. Speaking to the assembled crowds, he summed up the spirit of the occasion perfectly:

'It's a great honour and pleasure to be here today on this glorious occasion. My association is the Association of Railway Preservation Societies, of which the North Eastern Locomotive Preservation Group is a leading light. We do our best to weld together the vast volunteer effort and enthusiasm in our country. Welding volunteers together required a very special form of leadership and captain's stripes count for nothing! The majority of the locomotives in the Cavalcade belong to our members. Like all of our societies, the NELPG has never heard the word impossible, and Ian Storey and Maurice Burns, both of the North Eastern Locomotive Preservation Group, are two splendid representatives from our association members. These men refused against all odds to let steam die and often against a lot of establishment advice. They have rekindled the spirit of 1825 and are keeping it going strong. Long live steam.'

The next day, Tuesday 26 August, back at Thornaby, the

Prior to the exhibition at Shildon, some of the exhibits were put on public display at Darlington station. In the foreground are Nos 43105, 2005, 4498 *Sir Nigel Gresley*, 92220 *Evening Star* and MR No 1000 in what is now a car park. *John Hunt*

'P3' and 'T2' had two diesel-hauled running-in turns to Eaglescliffe. All was well. The fire was then lit in the 'T2', and the following day it hauled the 'P3' to Shildon via Darlington. The latter was still not complete mechanically, and indeed had not been steamed since its failure on the NYMR. As both engines entered the locomotive exhibition at Shildon Works Yard, it was quite an emotional moment and a huge sense of relief. The next day the 'P3' had its connecting rods fitted and was then steam tested, all to the satisfaction of BR. We had done it! All was now well and both engines, in addition to *George Stephenson*, were used on the Shildon passenger shuttles.

The day that had been in all enthusiasts' diaries for years then finally arrived – Sunday 31 August, the day of the Grand Steam Cavalcade. The sight of 35 engines all raising steam was unreal, as was the moment when all the engines saluted the 150th anniversary by blowing their whistles at 11am. The media were out in force, with Chris Lawson interviewed by Radio Tees and Maurice Burns interviewed by BBC TV *Look North*. Early mist was replaced by sunshine, as each engine

moved from the works yard to a big line-up, each carrying its position number in the Cavalcade, just as they had done in 1925.

Appropriately Nos 4767, 2238, 2392 and 2005 took their places as exhibits 3, 4, 5 and 6 behind *Locomotion*, leading the cavalcade, and NCB 'Austerity' 0-6-0ST No 2592/7. Crowds were everywhere, swelled by 20 charter trains from the south, the first of which arrived at 7.15am. Neither British Rail, nor the police, were prepared for the numbers of people who travelled from all over the North East, the UK at large, and abroad, to see the spectacle of the Grand Cavalcade. No one could ever have imagined the crowd scenes that witnessed the NELPG's four engines steaming from Shildon to Darlington. In all, 18,000 people paid to see the Cavalcade from the specially erected grandstands overlooking the line, but a massive 300,000 people took every vantage point along the route and watched it for free!

As the engines moved off, they each whistled at the crowds as they passed the grandstands and people clapped. It was truly a moment that the NELPG

With Captain Peter Manisty, the artist John Wigston and NELPG Technical Secretary Maurice Burns looking on, NELPG Chairman Ian Storey presents a painting of No 4767 to the Rt Hon William Whitelaw MP after the naming ceremony on 25 August 1975. *John Hunt*

After the dramas surrounding its appearance, and with its fire lit, 'P3' No 2392 keeps nocturnal company with GWR 0-6-0PT No 7752 and Caledonian Railway 0-4-4T No 419 in the yard at Shildon. *John Hunt*

During the week of celebrations, a series of shuttles ran from a specially built platform adjacent to the Masons' Arms level crossing for about a mile to a point beyond Shildon Junction. Each train was 'topped and tailed' with a locomotive at each end. Here No 2238 leaves the platform, with No 41241 on the rear. *John Hunt*

A view over the exhibition area at Shildon on the morning of 31 August 1975, with all the locomotives raising steam in readiness for the Grand Cavalcade. Centre stage are Nos 2238 and 4767, but also visible are Nos 7752, 51218, 6960 *Raveningham Hall*, 61306, 4498 *Sir Nigel Gresley* and 4771 *Green Arrow*. The early morning dullness soon gave way to clear blue skies and brilliant sunshine! *John Hunt*

No 4472 *Flying Scotsman* takes a back seat as Nos 4767 *George Stephenson*, 2238, 2392 and 2005 get the undivided attention of the watching crowds. *John Hunt*

The Grand Cavalcade was a proud day for the NELPG as each of its locomotives paraded past the vast crowds. Here No 2392 takes its turn. *John Hunt*

volunteers present at the event will never forget as Nos 4767, 2238, 2392 and 2005 all steamed by. It was undoubtedly one of the proudest days in the history of the Group.

The S&D 150 event was, of course, a great fillip to NELPG finances. The very active sales team, with the largest sales stand at the event, together with its associated photographic display, succeeded in raising more than £1,100 in six days. The general publicity provided the Group with considerable public exposure. This success was not limited to Shildon, for Nos 2238,

2392 and 2005 later went on exhibition at Stockton station from 20 to 27 September, where another £500 was raised. While there, the engines attracted no less a visitor than the then Prime Minister, the Rt Hon Harold Wilson MP. Grasping the opportunity, Chris Lawson presented him with a copy of the first edition of *North Eastern Revival*. While the Group's three locomotives basked in the exhibition, No 4767 ran under its own steam to Grosmont, to commence a new life, hauling trains on the NYMR.

After the Stockton exhibition the opportunity

Chris Lawson sells a 4767 first-day cover to Peter Manisty, ARPS Chairman, who had been instrumental in reducing the purchase price of the 'J27'. *John Hunt*

was taken to retain the 'T2', 'P3' and 'K1' at Thornaby roundhouse, to allow Teesside volunteers to tackle further mechanical work close to their homes. This was to be the final occasion that steam engines stood in Britain's last-built roundhouse. On 22 December 1975, the nostalgic sight of the three locomotives in adjoining roads in that building, against a beautiful sunrise, was duly photographed. As the engines departed from Thornaby for the last time, it brought to an end a year, and indeed an era, that will probably never be rivalled in the NELPG's history.

Above: Located in a prime position inside the Exhibition Hall, the NELPG photographic exhibition and sales stall took more than £1,100 during the week, an unprecedented amount in 1975. *John Hunt*

Right: On 27 September 1975 Nigel Bill, Alan Higgitt, John Whitbread, Ian Storey and Maurice Burns stand in front of *Locomotion* at Shildon following the presentation of special plaques to recognise the participation of the Group's locomotives at the S&D 150 celebrations the previous month. The National Railway Museum opened that same day*John Hunt*

10 GEORGE STEPHENSON AND THE NELPG

No story of the NELPG would be complete without reference to the link with engine No 4767. This was one of the legendary class of 842 'Black Five' mixed-traffic 4-6-0s designed by William Stanier and built by the London Midland & Scottish Railway and British Railways between 1934 and 1951. Without doubt this was one of the most successful designs produced by the LMS, the locomotives giving excellent Walschaerts valve gear, but for this experiment some locomotives were fitted with the Italian Caprotti valve motion, and one engine, No 4767, with outside Stephenson's valve gear, a design going back more than 100 years! Additional features comprised a double blast pipe and chimney, self-cleaning smokebox, rocking grate, hopper ashpan, and electric lighting.

The purpose of fitting Stephenson link motion

An official LMS works photograph of No 4767 as built with double chimney at Crewe in 1947.

and economical performance, as well as reliability and easy handling, making the class so versatile that they were just as much at home on 90mph expresses as they were on heavy freight trains, and could be seen at work from London to the north of Scotland. Though basically all of the same design, some members of the class incorporated special features, and No 4767 was one of these. It was one of a batch of 30 engines built in 1947 to the design of H. G. Ivatt, with experimental Timken roller bearings and various types of valve gear, in an attempt to keep these popular engines abreast of modern motive power developments, to increase their availability and reduce periods between shoppings, and to lessen the work of maintenance, servicing and inspection. The vast majority of the class incorporated

was to see what real advantage occurred from having variable lead. A characteristic of this valve gear is that the lead is increased by notching-up and this should have been of benefit when running at high speeds with short cut-offs, as the maximum amount of steam is enabled to enter the cylinder. No results from this experiment were published, and consequently no definite figures are available for comparison of the performance of this engine with that of a standard Class 5 4-6-0 locomotive fitted with Walschaerts valve gear. However, it is the general opinion that this engine compared very favourably with the others in the Class. It was a free runner and showed from experience a slightly improved performance on rising gradients, and also in accelerating from rest. However, one

No 44767, with a good head of steam, leaves Halifax with an evening express for Liverpool on 28 August 1961.
Gavin Morrison

No 44767 works hard at Bessie Ghyll between Penrith and Shap with the daily Carlisle-Willesden express freight
on 12 April 1967. It was fully-fitted but is running as a Class 4 rather than a Class 3 due to overweight.
Peter J. Robinson

consequence was the removal of the double chimney due to difficulties experienced with steam drifting down and tending to obscure the driver's view under the conditions in which this particular engine worked.

Following completion at Crewe, No 4767 was allocated to Bank Hall depot, Liverpool, for a number of years until transfer to Southport in April 1960. It was then moved to Carlisle Kingmoor depot in September 1963, from where it worked over both the Settle & Carlisle line to Leeds, and the West Coast Main Line over Shap until withdrawal from service on 30 December 1967 on the closure of Kingmoor depot to steam traction.

No 4767 was then purchased for preservation by the 45428 Stanier Class Five Locomotive Society Ltd and moved to the private steam centre at Carnforth for restoration. The catalyst for the return of the locomotive to working order was the S&DR 150th celebrations as described in the preceding chapter.

Following the Shildon celebrations, No 4767 went immediately to the NYMR and entered traffic, where it became a mainstay of the fleet as a regular and reliable performer. Having received its main-line ticket in 1975, it also made regular forays onto the main line, often on NELPG-sponsored railtours.

During 1980 NELPG volunteers and owner Ian Storey completed a full boiler retube of 4767 at Grosmont – see the picture in firebox on page 145. This enabled the engine to travel widely on the BR network. When the next boiler overhaul became due in 2002 it was more complex and as a result it was carried out at Ian Storey's workshop at Hepscott near Morpeth without NELPG involvement, thus bringing the happy involvement with 4767 to a close. It briefly returned to the NYMR in 2011, but then moved to the North Norfolk Railway in recent years. In total 4767 covered a huge 77,571 miles hauling NYMR passenger trains since it arrived in 1975 – a major contribution to the continued operation of the NYMR.

The unique Stephenson's link valve gear on No 44767, pictured at Carlisle Kingmoor, with No 60532, which had just worked in over the Waverley route, as company, on 8 October 1966. *John Hunt*

'Class 5' No 4767 *George Stephenson* was the natural choice for motive power for a George Stephenson Bicentennial Special trains that ran between Newcastle and Hexham on 6 June 1981. Organised jointly by BR and the Wylam Round Table four return trips took place and in this picture the special runs alongside the River Tyne on the approach to Hexham. *Maurice Burns*

No 4767 passes Carter's House on the climb from Levisham to Goathland Summit on the NYMR on 21 June 1981. *John Hunt*

The Group's association with the National Collection goes back to 1967 when the late John Scholes, then Curator of Historical Relics to the BR Board, was approached in connection with the possible loan of Raven's final freight locomotive design, Class 'Q7' 0-8-0 No 63460, then in store at Hellifield.

As mineral traffic continued to grow, the North Eastern Railway predicted a need for an even larger freight locomotive. In 1919 Raven produced a three-cylinder 0-8-0 of immense power derived from his successful Class 'Z' 'Atlantic' express engines. Railway companies had only limited need for such power and only 15 of Class 'T3' (LNER Class 'Q7') were produced. They served the railway best on one of the toughest tasks in the area, hauling iron-ore trains from Tyne Dock to Consett, 1,000 feet above sea level. On the steepest gradients (as much as 1 in 35 in places), 'Q7s'

'Q7' No 901 passes Cowton, between Darlington and Northallerton, with an up coal train at 3.08pm on 19 June 1920. *William Rogerson, Rail Archive Stephenson*

were to be found at both front and rear of 700-ton trains.

As NER 'T3' Class No 901, the stored locomotive was a fine example of the ultimate development of NER freight motive power and represented Britain's most powerful 0-8-0. The 'T3' was a natural progression from Raven's 'T', 'T1' and 'T2' 0-8-0 types, but one notable difference from the earlier engines was the additional cylinder, the drive from all three being on the second axle, whereas on the earlier two-cylinder engines the drive was on the third axle. The first of a batch of five 'T3s', No 901 was outshopped from North Road Works at Darlington in October 1919. Work would have commenced on it at the same time as 'T2' No 2238 was being completed. A further ten 'T3s' were built by the LNER in 1924.

Beginning on 10 November 1919, when the locomotive was only a few weeks old, extensive tests took place between Blaydon and Carlisle using No 901 and the NER dynamometer car, culminating on 14 November with a train weighing 1,400 tons, which No 901 hauled competently, making a clean start from rest

on the 1 in 298 rising gradient immediately west of Haydon Bridge station. In the opposite direction a load of 784 tons was started successfully on the 4 miles at 1 in 107 east of Wetherall. However, the trials that created most interest were those using locomotive No 903 on the North British Railway's Edinburgh to Perth line in 1921. On this occasion, the locomotive hauled a load of 755 tons up the 6 miles 53 chains at 1 in 75 of Glenfarg bank in 33 minutes, using full regulator and in full forward gear! Later, the same locomotive was used on dynamometer car trials between Newport and Shildon Yard, to establish the load that could be worked over the Simpasture branch in comparison with electric locomotives.

Initially No 901 went to Blaydon shed to work to Carlisle and south to York, but by December 1923 it was stationed at Hull (Dairycoates). There it was used for hauling train loads of empty mineral wagons to Gascoigne Wood Yard and the South Yorkshire pits, returning with loads of coal for shipment. It remained on this work until displaced by Government-surplus Class 'O4' 2-8-0 locomotives of Great Central design in 1927/28. Thus on 19 July 1929 No 901 was transferred back to the North East, spending the next 10 years at Haverton Hill, Stockton, West Hartlepool and Darlington. Under the massive wartime reallocation scheme implemented on 28 March 1943, all 15 'T3' locomotives were concentrated at Tyne

Dock shed to work the steeply graded route to Consett. No 901 was renumbered 3460 in October 1946, under the LNER renumbering scheme, becoming Class 'Q7' in the process, and No 63460 in October 1951. During that latter year No 63460 was fitted with vacuum brake equipment for work on the Tyne Dock-Consett iron-ore trains, and two Westinghouse pumps for opening and closing the air-operated doors on the specially built ore wagons, but it was the first to lose the latter in October 1957 when the 'Q7' locomotives became redundant on the Consett duty, being displaced by the new BR Standard 9F 2-10-0s, which were similarly fitted.

No 63460 was withdrawn from service on 3 December 1962, when all remaining members of the class were withdrawn en masse, but it had been announced late in 1960 that a 'Q7' locomotive was to be preserved to represent the ultimate design of 0-8-0 freight locomotive. Consequently, when No 63460 was withdrawn it was not cut up for scrap with the others of the class, but moved to Darlington Works for storage, pending the finding of a home.

Over the years, because of the absence of automatic brakes, the North Eastern 0-8-0s had only rarely been seen on passenger trains, and then only in a dire emergency where a train engine had failed and an eight-coupled locomotive was the only available alternative. It was therefore a day to remember on 28

No 63460 passes South Pelaw to begin the climb to Consett on 28 September 1963 with the RCTS 'North Eastern Limited'. *Armstrong Trust*

September 1963 when, after a full repaint at Darlington Works, No 63460 successfully worked the SLS/RCTS five-day tour special train from South Shields to Consett and from Consett to Bishop Auckland via Lanchester. Furthermore, on 2 May 1964 it worked the RCTS 'North Eastern Limited' special from Middlesbrough to Newcastle, via Wellfield. This proved to be No 63460's BR swan song, and the engine spent the next 13 years in store at Darlington, Stratford (London), Hellifield and, eventually, Preston Park at Brighton.

Following the initial approach in 1967, the Group kept in close contact with the Museum authorities, expressing its interest in the locomotive to increase the number of larger locomotives on the NYMR, until, in 1973, a small working party of Jeff Brand, John Hunt and Maurice Burns was allowed to carry out a visual examination of No 63460, making the long journey from the North East to Brighton. This examination revealed a boiler that had obviously had a general overhaul and done little work. Stay heads looked new, as did the smokebox and superheater elements. The full extent of how good the boiler was, in spite of being in store for nine years at North Road, Hellifield and Brighton, was brought firmly home when Maurice knocked out a boiler door to look at the foundation ring and got drenched! The boiler had never been drained since its last steaming on 4 May 1964 and was still full of water nine years later. Mischievously, they could nearly have lit it up! Mechanically it needed an overhaul, but the engine was basically sound, with all fittings intact.

'P3' No 2392 moves to the NRM

The NRM opened at York in 1975 occupying what had been York North motive power depot, home for many years to No 65894. During the discussions regarding the 'Q7', ties with the NRM were strengthened during 1977 when, following an approach from the museum, it was agreed to loan the 'J27', now in the guise of 'P3' No 2392 to York to represent the ubiquitous 0-6-0 goods engine, once the most common type of steam locomotive in Britain, but not represented in the National Collection. By coincidence, No 2392 needed retubing and was likely to have been out of NYMR service for some time, so it was mutually agreed on a loan period of three years. In readiness, the locomotive was completely repainted to exhibition standard by members, even the inside of the smokebox receiving a coat of paint! Following movement to York by low-loader on 17 October 1977, the formal handing over took place on 3 December, with a short ceremony witnessed by the Keeper of the Museum, Dr John

'P3' No 2392 sits proudly on the turntable inside the NRM at York in November 1977. *John Hunt*

Coiley, the Group's Chairman, Ian Storey, and a sizeable gathering of members. The 'P3' was the first steam locomotive purchased and restored by a voluntary organisation to be exhibited at the NRM; surrounded, but not overawed, by some of Britain's most famous steam locomotives, the 'P3' gave the Group and the NYMR invaluable publicity.

'Q7' loan agreement with the NRM

Following No 63460's eventual movement from Brighton to York, a formal agreement was reached between the NELPG and the NRM for a loan of the 'Q7' for ten years in the first instance, and for its overhaul to working order and subsequent operation. The Group, though, would have to finance the restoration. The Group felt honoured to be granted custody of this fine three-cylinder machine. A fund with a target of £3,000 was immediately launched in order to finance full retubing, mechanical overhaul and repainting.

In 1978 the 'Q7' was towed from York to Grosmont by preserved diesel No D5500, arriving on 7 April, and was initially stored at Goathland, but when Deviation shed was constructed by NELPG volunteers the 'Q7' became the first locomotive put under cover – a requirement of the loan. Due to the need to keep the 'K1', 'P3' and 'T2' in NYMR traffic and the 'K1' working railtours, the 'Q7' overhaul, which started in February 1980, could only progress when time allowed, as all work was done by volunteers and none was contracted out. Paul Smith, who had a passion for the 'Q7', was the driving force in getting the restoration started and urging volunteers to get involved. The axle box overhaul was overseen by the new expert Richard Campbell, while Maurice Burns oversaw the retubing and overhaul by NELPG volunteers. After reassembly and full repainting by Len Clarke in LNER livery as No 901, on the instructions of John Bellwood, now CME of the NRM, the first steaming took place on 18 July 1990. The 'Q7' entered traffic on 20 August that year and saw regular use on the NYMR until 1998, when it was withdrawn from traffic at the expiry of its ten-year boiler certificate, having covered 23,428

The 'Q7', minus boiler, is seen under repair inside the NELPG's Deviation shed in 1984, jacked up on packing for attention to the axle boxes, with Peter Hardcastle watching Richard Campbell trial-fitting an axle box and Kevin Buckle looking on. *Maurice Burns*

miles. Of interest to today's restorers of locomotive boilers is the fact that the engine ran its ten years in NYMR traffic using the BR Darlington North Road superheater elements, no boiler work was required, and the tubes fitted by NELPG volunteers lasted 10 years and are still in the locomotive to this very day!

As the Group was not in a financial position to carry out the necessary overhaul to renew the certificate, the 'Q7' was put on static display at Grosmont before responsibility for the engine was handed back to the NRM. Then, in full agreement with the Museum, at that time headed by former NELPG Committee member Andrew Scott, the locomotive was moved to Locomotion at Shildon, then to Head of Steam, Darlington's Railway Museum at North Road

Station, where it continues to be on public display.

Since Locomotion opened at Shildon in 2004, occupying the very spot where NELPG volunteers had relaxed after a busy exhibition week nearly 30 years before after watching the S&D 150 Cavalcade, the Group's links with the NRM have strengthened further. Since the opening of the museum, NELPG locomotives have been regular visitors and volunteers have served both organisations. The 'Shildon Shed Bash' at the end of July 2016 brought the iconic *Flying Scotsman* to the museum and saw 'J72' No 69023 heading the brake-van passenger shuttle with the 'A3', and 'Q6' No 63395 also in steam in the company of 'V2' No 4771 *Green Arrow* and 'A4' No 60009 *Union of South Africa*.

'Q7' No 901 heads out of Goathland with the NELPG's annual dining train in October 1990. *Maurice Burns*

12 THE SURPRISE PURCHASE OF '|72' No 69023 JOEM

At the other end of the motive power scale were the vast numbers of 0-6-0T shunting locomotives employed in goods yards and at coal staiths all over the North Eastern Railway system. They were quickly scrapped in the early 1960s, but one lucky survivor was privately preserved and, more than 20 years later, came up for sale. This is the story of how, in 1982, the NELPG was able to purchase Class 'J72' (NER Class 'E1') No 69023.

The class was introduced by Wilson Worsdell in 1898, based on the Class 'E' tank introduced 15 years earlier by Thomas Worsdell (elder brother of Wilson), who was CME of the NER from 1885 to 1890. With a reduced wheel diameter and increased cylinder size, the 'E1' had an increased tractive effort of 16,670lb as compared to the 12,130lb of the Class 'E'. A total of 113 were built between 1898 and 1951, all to the

original design, with the final batch costing £5,314 to construct. The last few must have made a strange contrast in Darlington Works alongside the up-to-date Ivatt 2-6-0s being produced at the same time.

Their basic tasks were shunting yards, stations, docks and coal staiths, and they could be seen at almost every location in the North East, although some ventured as far as Wrexham in Wales and Kittybrewster near Aberdeen. No 69023 was from the very last batch to be built in 1951, and, as its works plates indicate, it was the 2,151st locomotive to be built at Darlington North Road Works since building began in 1864. It spent its career allocated first to Darlington, then, in 1961, to Blaydon shed. Within seven years, however, scrapping of the class began, and six years later all 113 locomotives had been withdrawn except for two – Nos 69005 and 69023, condemned

No 69023, as Departmental No 59, stands in North Blyth roundhouse in 1966, *Bob Anderson*

in October 1964 but transferred into Departmental Service and renumbered 58 and 59 respectively.

At first the two were stationed at North Blyth and fitted with steam lances for use in de-icing coal wagons and points on Blyth coal staiths. They served only one winter on this task, however, and were then moved to Gateshead, where No 58 was tried (unsuccessfully) as a source of steam for cleaning diesel locomotive bogies and for de-icing points in Tyne Yard. A long period in store at Heaton followed, and No 59 was condemned for a second time in September 1966, but purchased for preservation the next month by Ron Ainsworth. No 58 was moved to Tyne Dock for storage, but the hope that it would also be preserved by two NELPG members was not realised, and it was condemned in October 1967 and scrapped.

Thus, on 13 September 1966, before the NELPG was founded, No 59 – with the hand-painted name *Joem* above the number (a combination of Ron Ainsworth's parents' names, Joseph and Emmeline) – was prepared for its journey in steam down the East Coast Main Line via Newcastle, Darlington and York (where it picked up Pullman Car No 84) to Leeds Holbeck. A wooden extension had been made to the coal rails to increase capacity for the journey. It stayed at Holbeck until 16 October, when it was steamed

again for its final journey to the Keighley & Worth Valley Railway (KWVR).

Repainted in North Eastern Railway livery, *Joem* was used on Santa specials and other duties between 1968 and 1970, covering 1,325 miles in this time. It starred in the BBC TV version of *The Railway Children* in 1968, and, with 'USA' tank No 72, hauled the special train up the branch line for passengers on the first ever NELPG railtour – 'The North Eastern' with *Flying Scotsman* – in June 1969, but was eventually stopped for retubing. No 69023 left the KWVR for the Yorkshire Dales Railway in 1975 but, with no work carried out, it was sold in 1977 to the Derwent Valley Light Railway (DVLR) at York, which retubed it and introduced a new steam passenger service on this private line. It was even passed for main-line running for scenes in York station for the film *Agatha* starring Dustin Hoffman and Vanessa Redgrave. However, this new life was only brief as the DVLR decided to end steam services in 1979 and sell off the land, causing the *Yorkshire Post* to carry the headline 'End of the line for Joem'. The DVLR was about to auction the locomotive when the former owner's son, Paul Ainsworth, decided to take up the family's option to buy it back and moved it to the National Railway Museum for storage prior to sale.

No 69023, on its journey from Newcastle to Keighley having collected Pullman Car No 84 at York, passes Shipley on 13 September 1966. *Robin Lush*

No 69023 calls at Oakworth
on the KWVR with a Santa
special in December 1969.
Maurice Burns

The 'J72' stands at Layerthorpe
on the Derwent Valley Light
Railway with a train for
Dunnington in August 1977.
Roger Bastin

No 69023, in LNER livery, propels matching vehicles over the River Ouse at York on 30 November 1977 during the filming of *Agatha*, reliving the days when a 'J72' *was* the York station pilot. *Roger Bastin*

On 4 December 1981 the engine was put up for sale by auction at Sotheby's in London, with a reserve of £25,000, but no offers were made near this figure. During 1982 several preserved railways became interested but, with its limited haulage capacity and high price, it was not sold. However, Maurice Burns had been following developments, and while the Group was fully committed with a 'J27', 'Q6' and 'K1', it was felt worth investigating whether a way could be found to secure the engine. So, following examination of No 69023 in the Annex at York, which showed that it needed a number of repairs, and a meeting in the NRM tearoom with Paul Ainsworth, the sale price was negotiated down from £25,000 to £10,250. Behind the scenes, and in parallel with these activities, Andrew Scott had been investigating grant aid for help in buying the 'J72' and secured a grant for £5,250 towards its purchase from the Science Museum. This news came just days before a planned EGM to authorise the locomotive purchase. The timing couldn't have been better, and when the 75 members at the EGM heard that the locomotive could belong to NELPG for just £5,000, the vote to buy No 69023 was unanimous. An appeal fund soon raised the purchase price and the locomotive became NELPG property on 20 November 1982.

Joem was moved by road from York to the NYMR in January 1983. Repairs and restoration to running

order were carried out in Grosmont repair shed and, during this process, the blast pipe was found to be heavily carboned up, reducing its diameter by nearly an inch. When the blast pipe was removed and decarboned, the casting fell apart and a new one had to be made. However, even with this setback the locomotive was steamed within four months of arrival on the NYMR. It was used on Gala days, but made its name on 23 September 1984 when the NYMR had no working engines and *Joem*, the only engine left, successfully worked the only passenger service – two round trips from Grosmont to Pickering. In late 1985 the engine needed a full overhaul and the Group had by now secured No 5 depot at ICI Wilton as its base, with its good volunteer support and the Government Manpower Services Commission Scheme. This Scheme funded the locomotive's overhaul, which included new side tanks, bunker, smokebox and front tube plate. Following a members' livery ballot, *Joem* was repainted in BR Station Pilot livery as worn by Nos 68723 and 68736 for carriage shunting duties at Newcastle and York stations from May 1960 until their withdrawal in the autumn of 1963. The overhaul was completed in 1987, and from that date it was resolved that it should be known by its BR number, but it was a lost cause and it has continued to be affectionately referred to as *Joem*!

From the outset, the diminutive 'J72' was not going

Minus boiler but with its new smokebox front and side tanks, the 'J72' is seen inside No 5 depot at ICI Wilton as Gordon Wells surveys the equipment in place to skim the slide valve faces. *Maurice Burns*

A general view inside No.5 depot at ICI Wilton in 1986, showing the major component parts of the 'J72', plus the 'Q6' tender. *Maurice Burns*

to play a major part in providing day-to-day motive power on the NYMR, but it came into its own on special days hauling goods trains, inspection saloons and short shuttles between Grosmont and Goathland or Pickering and Levisham, running nearly 5,000 miles. Being small and easily transported by road, *Joem* also became the flag-carrier for the Group and visited many other heritage railways around the country, from the North Norfolk in the east to the South Devon in the west, the Bo'ness & Kinneil in the north and the Swanage in the south, as well as the Great Western Society at Didcot and open days at Hartlepool Power Station and BR Thornaby. In 1996 the locomotive's boiler ticket expired and it was stored on display inside the Deviation shed at Grosmont. It eventually worked its way to the front of the overhaul queue and in 2004 was moved from Grosmont to the workshop at Hopetown, Darlington. Its overhaul was completed in the spring of 2010, at a cost of £150,000, with a grant from the Heritage Lottery Fund. It then moved to Locomotion, Shildon, for running in and acted as the Museum's operating locomotive for the rest of the year. Subsequently it went on its travels once more,

including to the Tanfield, Great Central and Colne Valley Railways, as well as returning to the NYMR for short spells. However, with the agreement of the NYMR, the 'J72' subsequently moved its home base to Darlington and now, under the dedicated care of Fred Ramshaw and his team, provides the steam motive power on the Wensleydale Railway each operating season, returning to Hopetown each winter for maintenance.

Following a visit to the Epping & Ongar Railway in the spring of 2015, a hole developed in the cylinder block. With the agreement of the insurance company, this was repaired by metal stitching and the fitting of cylinder liners, and the locomotive has worked satisfactorily subsequently. When its next overhaul is due, however, consideration will need to be given to the casting of a new replacement cylinder block to see *Joem* through to its 75th birthday and beyond. The purchase of this locomotive, when the opportunity arose in 1982, and its subsequent operation thanks to NELPG volunteers and locomotive caretakers, has undoubtedly given countless pleasure to many.

No 69023, fresh from overhaul, shunts *Blue Peter* into No 5 depot on 2 June 1987 in readiness for its own major overhaul. *Maurice Burns*

13 'Pacific' power – 'A4' No 60019 Bittern and 'A2' No 60532 Blue Peter

When the NELPG was formed it was never an ambition to do anything other than try to save two old locomotive types of the North Eastern Railway and, as earlier chapters indicate, the membership had to fight to achieve even that. However, fate and opportunity saw the Group bravely enlarge its locomotive ownership to include Nos 62005 and 69023, which its founders could never have anticipated. For the NELPG, already stretched with limited volunteer resources, to even dream of anything else was unthinkable, and nothing would have happened had it not been for a series of special circumstances, all coming together at the same time, leading to the NELPG's involvement with LNER 'Pacifics' *Bittern* and *Blue Peter*. Without these special

circumstances, the history of the NELPG and the two 'Pacifics' could have been so very different.

Away from the mundane world of mineral traffic, the North East also saw its share of the more glamorous world of main-line steam expresses. In the 1930s competition between the West and East Coast routes to Scotland led the London & North Eastern Railway's CME, Nigel Gresley, to produce a streamlined development of his successful 'Pacific' express locomotives. The 'A4s' were to handle many of the crack East Coast expresses for the next 25 years, until the advent of diesel power. The first of this type was No 2509 *Silver Link*, which was produced to haul the new 'Silver Jubilee' streamlined express between London and Newcastle in 1935. Subsequent batches

No 60019 *Bittern* poses at Perth prior to working the final 'A4' tour between Glasgow Buchanan Street and Aberdeen on 3 September 1966. *Peter J. Robinson*

No 60532 *Blue Peter* heads south from Stonehaven with the 13.30 Aberdeen-Glasgow train
on 27 July 1966. *Roger Bastin*

No 60532 is seen again near Carmont on 9 July 1966 with the 13.30 Aberdeen-Glasgow Buchanan Street service.
Note the immaculately manicured permanent way. *Roger Bastin*

Blue Peter climbs Honiton bank between Axminster and Exeter with an LCGB special from London Waterloo to Exeter on 14 August 1966. *Brian Stephenson*

No 60532 stands at Carlisle Kingmoor depot on 8 October 1966 after working in over the erstwhile Waverley route from Edinburgh. *John Hunt*

NELPG Chairman Maurice Burns and Secretary Dave Pennock witness Geoff Drury
signing the LNER collection hire agreement (covering *Blue Peter* and *Bittern*) on 24 October 1986. *John Hunt*

included a series named after birds and allocated to
more general express duties. *Mallard*, of course, was to
become famous when it broke the world speed record
for steam traction in 1938.

After the last war the engineer A. H. Peppercorn
was responsible for the LNER's last new steam
engine designs, including the 'A2' Class 'Pacifics'. No
60532 *Blue Peter* represents the final development of
the LNER 'Pacific'. With smaller wheels than earlier
examples, the 'A2s' were not as speedy as their
predecessors but they were nevertheless capable of
generating immense power. They were to be found
on East Coast Main Line expresses alongside the
'A4s', but are perhaps best remembered for their
work in Scotland, particularly on the heavily loaded
'Night Aberdonian' between Aberdeen and Edinburgh.
Both types were to end their days on services
between Glasgow, Edinburgh and Aberdeen. Following
withdrawal from BR service, No 60532 and another of
the 'A4' series, No 60019 *Bittern*, were acquired by the
late Geoff Drury, later to be an NELPG Vice-President.

After a period that saw both 'Pacifics' in open
storage at Walton Colliery near Wakefield, they were
moved to the Dinting Railway Centre. At Dinting the
Blue Peter Locomotive Society funded boiler work to

allow No 60532 to steam both there and at Didcot
in the early 1980s. It was during a steam-raising at
Dinting in 1984 that a 5¼-inch flue tube suddenly
imploded, wrapping itself round the element. This
brought an abrupt end to the engine's steaming days.
By chance, this incident coincided with a space in the
Manpower Services Commission Scheme at ICI Wilton,
and this led to Maurice Burns making contact with
the remaining members of the Blue Peter Locomotive
Society, the CME of Dinting, a meeting with the late
Geoff Drury, and a meeting with Dr Ian Pearce of ICI.
The latter confirmed that the Manpower Services
Commission (MSC) scheme could be extended to
cover *Blue Peter*, if the Group wished. Without the
scheme extension the NELPG could have done
nothing. All discussions were very positive and the plan
was endorsed by the NELPG Committee. This led to
a ground-breaking deal when both locomotives were
signed over to the NELPG on long-term loan on 24
October 1986. The aim was to restore *Blue Peter* to
main-line working order but, as there were already
two other 'A4s' in service, restoring *Bittern*, other
than cosmetically (as it required major repairs), was
considered to be outwith the Group's resources.

This agreement included the principle that the *Blue*

Bittern is seen during its conversion to *Silver Link* by the MSC team inside No 5 depot at Wilton in December 1987. Note the valencing under construction. *Maurice Burns*

Bittern, as No 2509 *Silver Link*, is flanked by Nos 4498 *Sir Nigel Gresley* and 4468 *Mallard* outside the National Railway Museum at York on 3 July 1988 to celebrate the 50th anniversary of *Mallard*'s world steam speed record of 126mph. Volunteers from the A4 Locomotive Society pose as the three drivers, and steam escapes from *Silver Link*'s drain cocks courtesy of No 4498! *Maurice Burns*

Peter restoration cost had to be separately funded in order not to distract from the financial responsibility the NELPG had for the engines it owned. With an estimate of just £55,000 to restore the 'A2' (in addition to the MSC scheme contribution), a public appeal, led by Dave Martin, was launched. It received a massive response, which included the donation of the remaining funds and best wishes of the Blue Peter Locomotive Society.

In the meantime an inspired suggestion by NELPG members Danny Fawcett and the late Bruce Pool was to restore *Bittern* as the first 'A4', No 2509 *Silver Link*, in silver livery, that locomotive having been scrapped in the 1960s. This cosmetic restoration was assisted by paint sponsorship from Dulux and a team of MSC workers, in addition to NELPG coordination, and included valancing enclosing its driving wheels, carefully measured from *Mallard* and fabricated by the MSC team.

The distinctive appearance of this silver streamliner formed an evocative reminder of the pinnacle of British express train operation in the days before car and airline competition. In 1988 the restoration was complete, and the 'A4' was handed over as No 2509 *Silver Link* in a ceremony on the turntable at York, with speeches by Brian Coldwell of ICI, Maurice Burns, and Dr John Coiley, NRM Keeper. *Silver Link* was then exhibited at the NRM, York, and positioned alongside Nos 4498 *Sir Nigel Gresley* and 4468 *Mallard* to celebrate the 50th anniversary of the latter achieving the world steam speed record of 126mph.

After a lengthy period on display at the NRM, the 'A4' went on display at the Stephenson Museum on North Tyneside. It was during this period that the Great Central Railway offered to restore the 'A4' to working order, and an NELPG/GCR agreement was drawn up and signed at the Stephenson Museum on 31 March 1994. After movement to Loughborough this

Alan Ramsey looks on as Dave and Richard Pearson work on *Blue Peter* inside No 5 depot in April 1990. Beyond the 'A2' is the 'K1' and its tender. The scale of the ICI facility can be clearly seen. *Maurice Burns*

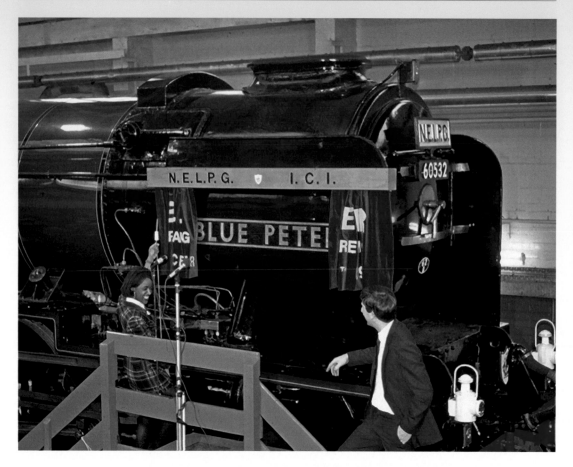

Diane-Louise Jordan, presenter of TV's *Blue Peter*, officially unveils the restored 'A2' at Wilton
on 11 December 1991 as Maurice Burns looks on. *John Hunt*

project faltered, which led to Geoff Drury deciding to
sell his 'A4' to Tony Marchington; at this point the 'A4'
was removed from the NELPG's responsibility. Today
Bittern is owned and operated by Locomotive Services
Ltd at Crewe.

NELPG members' attention then turned to the
overhaul of *Blue Peter* at ICI Wilton, and a programme
of work was agreed between the NELPG and the MSC
team, managed by Ken Thompson. This was to be the
biggest restoration ever done by NELPG volunteers
and was to be the very last major boiler repair that
the Group's volunteers ever did. Working parties were
on regular Monday and Thursday nights, with Terry
Newman looking after Mondays and Maurice Burns
Thursdays. David Pearson helped with coordination of
the MSC scheme on a day-to-day basis. To record this
historic restoration, a professional video record was
kept by NELPG member Ted Parker, from removing
the imploded flue tube to final painting and lining out
by Len Clarke. He then captured some magnificent
performances over the S&C line.

Throughout the restoration the press and regional
TV were regular visitors to ICI to conduct interviews,
and the BBC TV *Blue Peter* children's programme
attended ICI many times, which resulted in NELPG
volunteers being watched by millions! It was therefore
appropriate that on completion of the restoration on
11 December 1991, after speeches by Dr Ian Pearce of
ICI and Maurice Burns, the nameplate was unveiled by
BBC *Blue Peter* presenter Diane-Louise Jordan.

The engine then moved to the NYMR where,
after a successful test run, all the subscribers who had
funded the £55,000 overhaul travelled on a special
train to Pickering, where John Hunt presented the

Top right: No 60532 *Blue Peter* poses in superb ex-
works condition at ICI Wilton on the same day. *John
Hunt*

Bottom right: Blue Peter makes a splendid sight at Esk
Valley on the NYMR in December 1991. *Dave Rodgers*

driver and CME Maurice Burns with a certificate commemorating 25 years of NELPG volunteer service. There then followed seven days of continual NYMR running for the ex-works engine, without problems, before a loaded test run on BR early in 1992. There then began an extensive and far-reaching programme of railtours across the BR network.

The Durham wheel slip

This period of successful main-line running was abruptly interrupted by the Durham incident on 1 October 1994, when the outside valve gear was wrecked due to driver error when departing from Durham on the 'Heart of Midlothian' railtour from Edinburgh to York. In the public domain it is widely believed that the damage was purely due to a wheel slip, a not unusual occurrence on LNER 'Pacifics', but the whole cause was much more complex than that. What happened before the incident, during the Durham station departure, and the subsequent enquiry, is set out here for the first time.

Even before the Durham incident, crew error led to Blue Peter being involved in severe priming of the boiler when departing from stations such as Appleby, and there had been a very violent wheel slip when leaving Blackburn. As a result, the CME

was becoming increasingly nervous about BR crews and, just three days before the 1 October 1994 tour, took the precaution of establishing which named crew were rostered for the Edinburgh to York run. Satisfied with the names, all should have been well. However, 48 hours before the tour the crews were changed by RES in Crewe. No longer would it be the experienced men from Carlisle. The revised Blue Peter footplate crew ended up comprising a driver from Scarborough, who had never driven Blue Peter before, and a conductor driver from Newcastle who had never been on a steam footplate before, included because the Scarborough driver was not passed for the route. The inspector was from Darlington and the fireman from Thornaby. The Scarborough driver had been phoned by a York inspector about how to drive the engine: 'To get the engine into the big valve, put the reverser into mid-gear then open the regulator wide and let the reverser out.' Blue Peter's fate was sealed.

On the day itself, a tape recording of Blue Peter leaving Newcastle, southbound, showed that when the engine came off the King Edward Bridge and was heading towards Tyne Yard at 30mph on level track, the exhaust went silent as the regulator was shut, then, after a few seconds, there was a loud roar at the chimney. At Durham the situation was totally different, with a rising gradient of 1 in 120 and with

No 60532 accelerates across Durham Viaduct on 1 October 1994 on the 'Heart of Midlothian' railtour; seconds later it would slip for 35 seconds and destroy its motion. *John Hunt*

damp rail conditions. The train departed from Durham normally and the driver let *Blue Peter* gather speed to about 15mph as it crossed the viaduct. As it came off the viaduct the exhaust stopped as the regulator was shut, the reverser was put into mid-gear, the regulator opened wide and the reverser let out. As the wheels spun the driver struggled with the reverser and it flew into full forward gear, resulting in the wheels spinning at an estimated 140mph. It is most certain that the

engine primed. A normal wheel spin would last about 5 seconds, but this lasted a full 35 seconds – an eternity – before the regulator was shut, not by the driver, but by the fireman, who raced across the cab.

After the destruction of the motion, and with the ECML power isolated, NELPG volunteers, heroically led by Richard Campbell and working in dark conditions, disconnected and made safe the motion for the train to be towed back to Durham station. In view of the

The severely bent radius and eccentric rods on the left-hand side of the 'A2' are seen in October 1994 at Thornaby. *Maurice Burns*

An inspector accurately checks how much the wheel had moved on the crank axle in October 1994. *Maurice Burns*

Blue Peter's shattered radius rods. *Maurice Burns*

seriousness of the incident, CME Maurice Burns took the entire footplate crew, including Ian Pearson, NELPG footplate representative, and Terry Newman, Locomotive Responsible Officer, into a closed compartment and interviewed them. The report was passed to the British Railways Board, which convinced it of the urgent need to conduct its own inquiry.

After calls by the NELPG for compensation, the British Railways Board Special Trains Division held an internal inquiry at Euston, London. The inquiry was chaired by Steve McColl, Director of Special Trains, with Ian Pearson and Maurice Burns representing the NELPG, together with engineers, union officials, and the footplate crew. All those on the footplate were interviewed, including Ian Pearson. Video of the wheel slip was shown. The thorough inquiry and subsequent 40-page report led to a conclusion and compensation offered as per the following letter dated 24 March 1995:

volunteer time, and the loss of earnings by the engine, during the period of the repair, and the NELPG was never compensated for any of this. Without doubt, the British Railways Board got off lightly.

Eventually the 'A2' was repaired and, thankfully, resumed its main-line running, but only after the NELPG had produced a video of the multiple valve regulator, which all crews had to see.

One of the many highlights of this last period on the main line was the Edinburgh to King's Cross run that coincided with the 40th anniversary of the BBC *Blue Peter* programme. At the expiry of its main-line ticket in 2001, the 'Pacific' went back to the NYMR to work out the final few months of its boiler ticket, and was finally withdrawn from service on 3 November 2002, having run a total of 21,426 miles on the preserved line. It then went on static display, first at North Road Museum, Darlington, then Barrow Hill roundhouse, Chesterfield. As it was not possible

'Dear Maurice

Damage to Blue Peter 1/10/94

Thanks for your continued patience while we bring the inquiry to a conclusion. The panel found that at least 75% of the damage to the locomotive was as a direct result of the severe wheel slip that occurred as a result of the driver not being given adequate revision training.

We will therefore accept we will pay 75% of the costs for the repairs to the locomotive as evaluated by Mr K. Sargent and you can invoice us for £37,586 and British Rail will also cover the costs of a test run when due.

Yours sincerely

Steve McColl'

Although it looks on the surface to be a fair result, the letter masked the real difficulty faced by the NELPG. In an ideal world, the locomotive would have been passed over to a major contractor to be sorted out, but no such contractor existed at that time. NELPG volunteers had to tackle it, but with two engines, the 'J27' and the 'K1', under major overhaul, the volunteer CME was overstretched. This led to Paul Hutchinson coordinating the rebuild and the work being done at Thornaby over a two-year period. A contractor's cost, if one had been available, would have been more than £300,000. In addition, there was the huge amount of

to come to an agreement with the Drury family for a further period in main-line service, the locomotive was finally acquired by the Royal Scot Locomotive & General Trust, based at Crewe, where in 2016 it was undergoing a full overhaul.

The NELPG's love affair with 'Pacific' power is now over, but neither the generosity of steam enthusiasts who funded the overhaul, ICI who provided the restoration base, nor the restoration work entirely done by volunteers will ever be forgotten. Neither will the engine's immense power, being one of Britain's most powerful steam locomotives.

A cornerstone of the NELPG's past 50 years has been its appetite to run its steam locomotives on the main line for the sheer kudos and enjoyment, and for fund-raising. In recounting the depth and range of the Group's railtours, there are many stories to tell relating to locomotives, operating events and passenger experiences. Mainly it's about people making things happen, meeting deadlines and delivering on the day. There have been ups and downs of course, but the Group's resilience has always shone through in running its own trips and hiring out its locomotives to other railtour operators. Within the NELPG, a railtour team developed including John Hunt and Andrew Scott as organisers, Maurice Burns as Technical Secretary, then CME, Peter J. Robinson dealing with bookings, and Dave Pennock as tour manager. On-board sales were dealt with by the Brown family, while Peter and Pauline Robinson and Colin and Miriam Hatton handled telephone bookings, and latterly Bryan Orange managed tour publicity.

It all started in 1969 with the hire of *Flying Scotsman* from Alan Pegler, which at the time was the only steam locomotive authorised to operate on British Railways. This first railtour, on 29 June, was No 4472's last run before being shipped to the United States. It ran a circular route from Newcastle via York to Keighley, then via Colne, Preston and Carlisle. At Keighley the passengers enjoyed a run behind *Joem* and 'USA' tank No 72 – little did anyone know that *Joem* would ultimately become part of the NELPG collection! The first prize in the raffle was to be a footplate experience on *Flying Scotsman*, but the raffle tickets had been forgotten! A quick phone call by Richard Wheeler at Darlington resulted in tickets being delivered at one of the railtour stops, thus saving the day.

The NELPG's first railtour was on 29 June 1969 and featured *Flying Scotsman* from Newcastle to Keighley and back to Newcastle via Shap; it is pictured here at Greenholm on the climb to Shap summit. *Roger Bastin*

Newcastle's Central station even had a platform indicator board dedicated to the 'North Eastern' tour of 29 June 1969; note the ticket collector's booth.
Maurice Burns

The 'K1' and *George Stephenson* on the main line

A pent-up wish to see main-line steam saw a change of heart by BR, and in 1971 several secondary routes were approved for a select band of Class 7 and 8 locomotives. All this was pretty irrelevant to the NELPG with its Class 5 locomotives based on the NYMR. Then came a chink of light in 1975 when the Stockton & Darlington Railway celebrations allowed some Esk Valley steam runs, and the 'K1' hauled two Newcastle to Whitby tours. When the 1976 list was published, Nos 2005 and 4767 were still there! So it was that they became the first heritage-railway-based locomotives within the main-line fleet.

From 1976 the NELPG began to run regular railtours. Unlike some of the other loco owners, who were just glad to see their locomotives on the main line, the NELPG's aim was unashamedly to raise funds for its locomotives. Rolling stock for these first tours was a Heaton-based rake of 64-seat TSO coaches. The 1976 tour from Newcastle to Scarborough using Nos 4767 and 92220 *Evening Star* carried a massive 723 passengers, at the time a record for a main-line tour.

Subsequent tours saw the 'K1' run down the

With the Abbey and the River Esk as a backdrop, No 2005 leaves Whitby for Battersby with its first ever main-line trip on 8 June 1975. *John Hunt*

With the village cricket team in action in the distance, No 2005 departs from Glaisdale for Battersby with a return excursion to London St Pancras on 28 June 1975. *Chris Gammell*

No 2005 swings left off the King Edward Bridge at Gateshead with 'The Metro Express' from Newcastle to Middlesbrough on 4 September 1977. Note the now replaced Redheugh Bridge and the brightly coloured pigeon crees. *John Hunt*

Glimpsed between rows of miners' houses, the 'K1' heads south at Easington, on the Durham coast, with the same railtour. *John Hunt*

coast from Newcastle to Middlesbrough on a Metro Radio charter to Whitby in 1977, and in 1978 the 'Moorlander' tour had the 'K1' up the coast to Newcastle and 'A4' No 4498 *Sir Nigel Gresley* hauling it from Carlisle to Leeds. The 1978 'North Eastern' tour, with a new record of 736 tickets sold, had an incredible variety of steam, diesel and electric traction: 'K1' No 2005 Newcastle-Stockton. A 'Deltic' No 50022 *Royal Scots Grey* to York, 'V2' No 4771 *Green Arrow* to Dinting, two Class 76s, Nos 76030 and 76014,

to Tinsley Yard, Sheffield, with the 'Deltic' taking the train back north.

Into the 1980s, No 4767 hauled two 'Tyne-Tay' expresses between Newcastle and Carlisle, with photo stops at Haltwhistle, and 'A4' No 60009 *Union of South Africa* booked for Edinburgh to Dundee. Regrettably No 60009 did not make the first run; a 'Deltic' substituted, and Group members called at Markinch to inspect the 'Pacific', but embarrassingly it was clearly not a runner, and everyone received £1 compensation!

Despite the presence of a solitary policeman and a number of orange-clad stewards, passengers swarm all over the tracks to photograph No 4767 at Haltwhistle whilst on the NELPG Tyne-Tay Express on 19 April 1980. *John Hunt*

'K1' No 2005 pilots 'Black Five' No 4767 *George Stephenson* round the curve south of Armathwaite with the Group's 15th anniversary railtour on 24 October 1981. *John Hunt*

No 2005 makes a splendid sight at Long Marton with a southbound 'Northumbrian Mountain Pullman', loading to no fewer than 11 vehicles, on 22 January 1983. *Peter J. Robinson*

Sales on the first tour grossed some £600, driven by the sale of 'George Stephenson Lives' T-shirts. The second tour was marred by the 'A4' developing a tender hot box prior to the Tay Bridge, and the train was diesel-hauled back to Edinburgh.

Railtours are often tense affairs, as success depends upon a trouble-free locomotive. While hauling the 'Northumbrian' along the Tyne Valley in December 1980 No 4767 suffered a blowback in the cab due to a fractured blower pipe. Rear assistance was initially provided by a following Class 47 diesel, and the train subsequently reached Carlisle hauled by a Class 26 diesel. Not to be defeated, No 4767 was taken to Upperby shed, the defect repaired by Ian Storey, and a spirited run southbound was completed over the Settle & Carlisle line without further incident.

The bicentenary of George Stephenson's birth was commemorated in 1981 with No 4767 hauling four shuttles between Newcastle and Hexham. Also during the year the Group's 15th anniversary tour saw a combination of Nos 4747 and 2005 triumphantly double-heading a Middlesbrough-Skipton tour over the S&C line. By all accounts it was a close-run thing with herculean efforts by Maurice Burns and his team working into the early hours at Thornaby to ensure that the tour had its steam locomotives.

In 1983, under SLOA auspices, the 'K1' ran

Now with nine rather than 11 vehicles, the 'K1' makes steady progress up the 'Long Drag' at Horton-in-Ribblesdale on 20 March 1983 with the northbound 'Northumbrian Mountain Pullman'. *Ted Parker*

No 2005 passes Grangetown with a 'Saltburn Flyer' on 16 August 1986. The South Bank blast furnaces in the distance have since been demolished. *John Cooper Smith*

two NELPG tours hauling its Pullmans over the S&C. It was always an uphill battle to include the 'K1' in the SLOA railtour programme due to its limited haulage capacity and 50mph maximum speed. The first Pullman rapidly sold out and a second tour was run some eight weeks later. The 'K1' remarkably hauled some 405 tons unassisted over Ais Gill, a massive triumph, but it was a laboured performance. The second tour was therefore limited to nine vehicles. A more local affair was four return trips between Middlesbrough and Shildon to commemorate the 150th anniversary of the Shildon wagon works, when more than 1,000 passengers were carried.

As more steam routes were approved by BR, the NELPG's railtour horizons expanded. In October 1983 a Middlesbrough to Aberdeen full tour ran with No 60009 from Edinburgh to Aberdeen via the Forth and Tay bridges. BR had concerns over the weight of the 'A4' on the Tay Bridge and structure clearances near Aberdeen, but late in the day a series of 5mph restrictions allowed it to run. In 1984, unusually, 'Black Five' No 5407, deputising for No 4767, hauled a Group tour between Kilmarnock and Hellifield, returning it from Fort William. More locally, in 1986 the 'K1' ran

from Newcastle to Saltburn as the 'Saltburn Flyer' as part of the town's 150th anniversary celebrations.

With Scotrail opening up the Mallaig line to steam, the NELPG grasped the opportunity in 1987 to use the 'K1' on railtours associated with its moves to and from Fort William. The locomotive's return from Fort William to Edinburgh in 1988 was bedevilled by pre-tour concerns over fire risk and having to detach the support coach at Tulloch with a hot axle box. With true irony, the train ran over Rannoch Moor in a blizzard!

Two packed 'K1' specials, marketed as possibly the last trains up Weardale, in March 1993, ran from Darlington to Stanhope. At the time special permissions were required to run 'under the wires' at Darlington and to traverse the freight-only line to Eastgate.

'A2' 'Pacific' No 60532 *Blue Peter*

In 1992 the NELPG joined the 'Big Engine' club running, the 'A2' between Blackburn and Carlisle on 7 March. A second tour, satisfying a strong demand for the locomotive, ran on the 21st from Carlisle to Bradford Forster Square. In the capable hands of the

No 60532 *Blue Peter* effortlessly tops Ais Gill summit southbound on 20 June 1992. *John Cooper Smith*

The magnificent spectacle of No 60532 in full cry at Birkett Common, south of Kirkby Stephen, with the NELPG's 'Waverley' rail tour on 6 March 1993. *John Cooper Smith*

'Blue Riband' crew Driver Willie Alexander, Fireman Paul Kane and Inspector Jimmy Baker, this tour proved to be a classic. Leaving Carlisle some 49 minutes late and with speeds of 70mph-plus, 16 minutes were clawed back by Appleby. Despite easing off because the injectors had difficulty in maintaining water level because of the high demand for steam, the Appleby to Ais Gill record held by No 71000 *Duke of Gloucester* was only missed by 16 seconds – clearly we had a thoroughbred in our midst. *Blue Peter*'s popularity continued, such that the 6 March 1993 'Waverley' tour, running northbound over the Settle & Carlisle line, was fully booked in three weeks. A run on 6 May between York and Scarborough for the SRPS had BR scratching its head as the electrical clearances under the footbridge over Platforms 3 and 5 at York were judged too tight for steam. With the help of John Frankish (BR) and Norman Hugill (SLOA), approval was finally granted and the trip ran successfully.

Given *Blue Peter*'s BR working life on Glasgow to Aberdeen services, a key aspiration of the Group was to take the 'A2' back to its old stamping grounds and return to Aberdeen. Its initial return to Scotland

came during the Group's 'Fair Maid' tour in September 1993, with the 'A2' being attached at Carlisle, running outward to Perth via Stirling and returning via the Forth Bridge to Edinburgh Waverley. One month later the return of the 'A2' to Aberdeen was arranged for Sunday 17 October. The Group was to use the SRPS stock following its previous day's use on a charter hauled by 'Black Five' No 44871 returning from Fort William. Well, that was the plan, but the weather had other ideas. The 'Black Five' running to Glasgow was beset by poor autumnal rail conditions such that the stock for the tour was not readily available for the early-morning departure. To compound matters, a harsh overnight frost, despite a beautiful morning sun, had left patches of icy rail on the 1 in 75 Dunfermline Bank, and No 60532 just could not find its feet. The train had to be ignominiously rescued by diesel No 56104 dispatched from Thornton depot, and the train arrived in Perth some 3 hours late. There it was turned round at Perth, the Group promising to have another go at reaching Aberdeen.

The 'North Eastern' railtour in May 1994 used both the 'K1' and the 'A2' on a York to Skipton

Reflecting the setting sun, No 60532 climbs from Grangemouth Junction, Falkirk, to Polmont with the ill-fated 'Aberdonian' on 17 October 1993. *John Hunt*

Coming home! In glorious summer weather, *Blue Peter* crosses the Esk Viaduct at Montrose with the returning 'Aberdonian' on 21 August 1994. *Pamela Marriner*

itinerary, the 'K1' working the Darlington-Carlisle leg and the 'Pacific' providing the traction from Carlisle to Skipton, with two run-pasts at Appleby. The 'K1', hauling 12 bogies and running under the then new ECML wires, was seen as a milestone in itself. Unusually and regrettably, one passenger was the worse for drink, and became aggressive after stealing some wine from the dining car at Skipton. Sensing matters were not going to get any easier, British Transport Police were called. A diminutive WPC met the train in Carlisle, calmly summoned the passenger and he immediately complied. Unbelievable!

The second attempt to reach Aberdeen on 21 August 1994 proved to be a resounding success, although the 'A2' suffered some damage from a slip due to priming on an SLOA charter near Blackburn in July and middle cylinder repairs had to be completed prior to hauling the 'Aberdonian'. On the day the sun shone and once again an 'A2' triumphantly ran into Aberdeen. The smiles all around said we had done it!

Running steam on the main line is a combination of ecstasy and agony. Riding on the ecstasy of Aberdeen, the agony hit us all at Durham on 1 October 1994. The tour was a return move of Blue Peter from Scotland with a planned ECML run from Edinburgh to Darlington. As already recounted in the previous chapter, on departure from Durham control of the engine was lost, causing a catastrophic slip, wrecking the locomotive's motion in the process. The stranded train blocked the ECML for some 2 hours and the incident became a low point of our main-line running, although the NELPG was not at fault. Rebuilding the 'A2' demonstrated the call to arms and resilience of the restoration team, which was rewarded by the NELPG subsequently winning the ARPS Annual Award.

Blue Peter triumphantly returned to the main line in 1996 by hauling a 'North Briton' tour on 23 November. Nonetheless, the tour did have its problems when the empty stock train from London arrived 2½ hours late in Middlesbrough. This initial lateness was never recovered and the S&C running was via moonlight, with arrival back in Middlesbrough just before 23.00! EWS put its hands up for the delays and a full refund of its charges was made to the NELPG in compensation.

Approaching the end of its seven-year main-line certification, the Group's possible final 'A2' tour ran from Middlesbrough to Preston via Gateshead and Carlisle in September 1997. Despite being 16 minutes late away from Middlesbrough, with lively running along the Tyne Valley, Carlisle was reached 11 minutes early. A storming 64mph run over Shap turned a 3-minute-late departure from Carlisle into a 9-minute-early arrival at Lancaster. However, on arrival at Preston the expected Class 47 diesel was still at Carlisle, ultimately making the tour nearly 2 hours late home. Organising and running railtours is never for the faint-hearted!

Unusually, the next NELPG tour, the 'Irish Mail', ran from London Euston, using the 'A2' between Crewe and Holyhead. The bookings were relatively poor, but operationally the passengers were rewarded with speeds of 70-75mph along the North Wales coast.

Following a series of Spring 1998 tours, including visits to London and Edinburgh, the NELPG tour on 30 May acted as a 'thank you' to ICI, where the 'A2' had been restored. With an out-and-back over the ECML and the S&C line, Blue Peter ran in both directions over Ais Gill. Southbound it was joined by No 60007 Sir Nigel Gresley to enable both locomotives to reach Doncaster for a display celebrating the 60th anniversary of Mallard's world speed record.

To extend Blue Peter's boiler certification, a retube was completed by Ian Storey during 1998, but before the engine could return it had to prove that its spark arrestors were efficient. This was done on an empty stock night test run preceding a public run from Hellifield.

Sadly, Geoff Drury, the locomotive's owner and NELPG Vice President, passed away in late 1999 and a memorial train from York to Preston via Carlisle was run for him on 8 April 2000. The 'A2' was humorously adorned with 'Albatross' nameplates, reflecting his pet name for the engine. The train's promotion included telephone bookings and it was advertised on the internet for the first time. The 'A2' performed well, but the train suffered delay at Low Fell due to it fouling the main line and the water tanker not being in the right place! Despite the often late receipt of timings, running the tours more than compensated for such stresses and strains. It is worth noting two comments from that day's tour. A rather perplexed coal loader at Carlisle, waiting for Blue Peter but who had just seen Albatross, was advised that 'the booked engine failed on shed and we had to take another one'! Equally, wit Steve Alder was heard to remark, 'I don't know who this Albert Ross fellow is, but he's got a bloody good engine!'

Excellent performances were also achieved in 2000 on tours over Shap, and for good measure the 'A2' also reached Swansea, Plymouth and King's Cross. Sales on these trains raised many thousands of pounds for the NELPG. By now Blue Peter was beginning to show its age with superheater tube leaks. Support crews, often working through the night, blanked off offending elements to ensure that the train ran. Subsequently the tubes were replaced and in early 2001 the 'A2' notably visited Bath, Bristol and Blackpool.

The Group's final Blue Peter tour ran on 9 June 2001. Running from Newcastle, the 'A2' joined the train at Crewe. With Driver Bill Andrew and Fireman Frank Santrian at the controls, Carnforth was reached some 15 minutes early. Passing Tebay at 74mph, Shap was crested with a full regulator, 30% cut-off and 210psi on the clock, reaching Carlisle 30 minutes early. Close to the end of the tour, at Durham, Blue Peter's chime whistle wailed out over the city. Arrival at Darlington was naturally emotional for all, as Blue Peter's main-line running in the hands of the NELPG had come to an end.

The final 'K1' tours

The 'K1' once again became the NELPG's flagship locomotive, and railtours concentrated on moving it to and from Fort William. On 8 June 2003 a Middlesbrough to Carnforth charter ran via Stockton, Ferryhill, the Tyne Valley and Shap – quite different from *Blue Peter*, but nonetheless the Group had run its diminutive 'K1' over Shap on a railtour. It had to wait until 2007 for the next tour, on 12 May, commemorating the 40th anniversary of the Stephenson Locomotive Society's 'Three Dales Tour' of 20 May 1967. The train reached Bishop Auckland, Crag Hall and Redmire in one day, and passed through Darlington and Middlesbrough on four occasions! The Bishop Auckland residents were, however, surprised by a drop in their morning water pressure as the 'K1' took water from a nearby hydrant. Traditionally, Martin Lloyd's culinary delights, splendidly prepared in the support coach kitchen, ably fed the support crew and the stewards.

In 2008 the 'North East Explorer' poignantly took the 'K1' past the Philips Refinery where in 1967 it had acted as a stationary boiler. The highlight of the day was visiting the Boulby potash mine, 50 years since the Middlesbrough-Whitby coast route closed to passengers. The 1 in 61 climb out of Boulby had the 'K1' at full stretch with its nine coaches and a dead No 47760 at the rear. Following a slip, close to a flange lubricator, the train stalled. The plan was for the Class 47 to assist if necessary, but only after coming to a stand did the diesel driver help – communication! The final raffle prize, a lump of 'K1' coal, caused some angst as it was won by a young girl and her disappointment had to be overcome by a selection of sweets from the buffet!

The 'North Eastern Mountaineer' on 4 May 2009 gave the 'K1' a return run over the S&C line with speeds of 25/30mph over Ais Gill, despite being halted at Kirkby Stephen with reports of sheep on

During the 'North East Explorer' tour from Middlesbrough on 10 May 2008, which took in Tyne Yard, Hartlepool and Seal Sands, No 62005 also visited Boulby and is pictured climbing up to Hunt Cliff from Skinningrove with the North Sea in the background. *John Hunt*

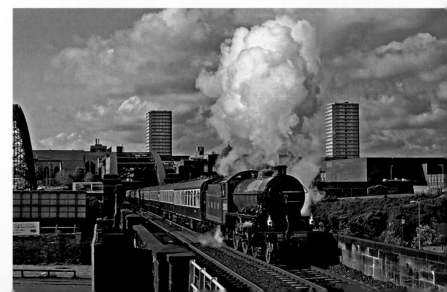

No 2005 approaches Monkwearmouth station with the 'Tees Clyde Express', having left Sunderland and crossed the River Wear via the bridge in the background on 13 June 1987. The 'K1' worked from Middlesbrough through to Kilmarnock via Newcastle and Carlisle. *John Hunt*

In BR livery No 62005 is seen at Bedale with the NELPG's re-enactment of the SLS 'Three Dales' tour of 1967 on 12 May 2007, returning from Redmire to Northallerton almost 40 years to the day. *John Hunt*

Nos 61994 *The Great Marquess* and 62005 cross the River Tees at Yarm on 9 November 2007 with the 'Tees Don Express' from Eaglescliffe to Barrow Hill, near Chesterfield. *Dave Rodgers*

No 62005 crosses the River Swale at Morton-on-Swale between Northallerton and Bedale with the RTC 'Wansbeck' railtour on 21 March 2015. *David Warren*

the line. The raffle raised £850 and, overall, the tour contributed £10,000 to Group funds. This was the NELPG's 35th tour and marked the 40th anniversary of the first railtour in 1969.

Last, but not least, in May 2010 the Group promoted the 'K1' to North Blyth, where it had been allocated in 1966. Well, that was the plan, but the engine had other ideas, and it had to be failed during the evening prior to the tour due to a cracked right-hand cylinder. It is a railtour operator's worst nightmare having to provide sincere apologies to 500 disappointed passengers.

At the time the Group did not know it, but this proved to the last NELPG-sponsored tour in its 50-year history. Because of the commercial risks involved for such an organisation, it was decided to promote

no more tours, but to continue to make the 'K1' available to other operators. Looking back over 41 years, NELPG locomotives have operated on railtours the length and breadth of Great Britain. The trials and tribulations have been a true test of the support crews, the planners and the train stewards concerned. The tours have equally raised countless thousands of pounds for Group funds and provided the untold pleasure of main-line steam. Wonderful!

London Underground's 'Steam on the Met'

'Steam on the Met' was inaugurated in 1989 and, as the event proved a great success, in the following year an event was staged running steam trains between Harrow-on-the-Hill and Amersham.

With Wembley's twin towers as a backdrop, No 62005 stands outside the shed at Neasden in the company of 'B12' No 61572 and No 41298 in May 2000. *John Hunt*

Above: No 62005 heads up the 1 in 106 at Chorleywood in May 1999. *John Hunt*

Left: A driver's-eye view from No 62005 at Amersham in May 2000. *John Hunt*

Opposite top: Left to right: Ian Pearson, Malcolm Simpson and Martin Lloyd with No 62005 at Ruislip LUL depot in May 1999. *John Hunt*

Opposite bottom: The 'K1' speeds through Chalfont & Latimer station between Rickmansworth and Amersham in May 2000. *John Hunt*

In the same month 'B12' No 61572 and No 62005 enjoy some spirited parallel running between Harrow-on-the-Hill and Watford South Junction, one of the highlights of 'Steam on the Met'. *John Hunt*

'Steam on the Met' then continued for the next few years, with services running from Amersham to Watford, using the little-used north curve at Rickmansworth. Crowds flocked to the events each year, which were logistically complicated for London Underground, as it had to run the steam services in between the normal Metropolitan and Chiltern services.

A special set of coaches was acquired and facilities provided at Neasden for the steam locomotives. Amersham became very busy, as it was used to change the steam locomotives on each train, which involved a number of train movements in and out of the sidings. Coaling and water facilities were also provided at Amersham. The event was manned by volunteers. A feature of many of the events was the parallel running along the fast lines from Harrow-on-the-Hill to Moor Park of two steam-hauled trains on the early and late trains to and from Neasden.

No 62005 was invited to take part in 1999 and 2000, crewed by NELPG drivers and firemen, and the 'K1' acquitted itself well. It was no mean task since, on getting the right away from Rickmansworth, it was hell for leather up the 6½ miles of uncompromising 1 in 106 gradient all the way to Amersham in order not to delay any following Chiltern or LUL trains!

Fort William-Mallaig

Since 1987 the 'K1' has participated in the highly successful Fort William-Mallaig operation, where it has excelled and been the most used locomotive; this is quite appropriate, as it is a classic case of 'horses for courses'. Ironically No 62005 carries the boiler from classmate 62011, which was one of the 'K1s' that went to the West Highland line when new. The 'K1' first participated in 1987, then in 1988, 1990, 1992, 1994 – the West Highland centenary year – 2001 to 2010 and 2012 to 2016. In all, the locomotive has spent 20 seasons on the West Highland Extension, more than any other locomotive.

Rated one of the 'Great Railway Journeys of the World', the Road to the Isles is a superb showcase for the 'K1', which is more than well suited to the demands of the line's sharp curves and fierce gradients. The latter can be as steep as 1 in 45 and can be quite a challenge, especially when the weather is inclement, which, in this part of the Scottish Highlands, can be quite often!

The logistics of this operation should not be underestimated, however. Since its first season in 1987, the NELPG has provided a support crew of up to four people each alternating operating week to maintain

No 62005 is captured in the classic setting of Glenfinnan Viaduct on 16 October 1994. *John Cooper Smith*

and prepare the locomotive for more than 70 days of main-line running in each season. They are responsible for raising steam in the morning, oiling round, cleaning the locomotive, watering the tender on arrival at Mallaig and, on the evening return to Fort William depot, cleaning the fire, adding water treatment to the tender as it is refilled, and carrying out any repairs after the locomotive has been examined. This can involve a 12-hour day and up to 10 days away from home at a time, a tall order for volunteers, and, as if this were not enough, the Fort William base is several hundred miles from volunteers' homes and from the Group's stores and workshops. To provide volunteer transport to, from and around Fort William, the NELPG has operated its own support car for several years.

Since joining the main-line pool in 1975, up to 2016 the 'K1' had made more than 1,000 trips on the main line, amassing a total of more than 113,000 miles in the process, with excellent reliability – a great credit to all those involved.

Against a setting once described by iconic Scottish photographer W. J. V. Anderson as 'Wagnerian', No 2005's fireman prepares for the climb off Loch nan Uamh Viaduct up to Arnabol and Polnish with a Mallaig-Fort William train on 11 September 1994. *John Cooper Smith*

No 2005 heads towards Corrour in March 1988. Every picture tells a story, and all is not as it seems! The 'K1' was en route *to* Fort William, yet here it is heading towards Glasgow. The opportunity to photograph the 'K1' in the snow was not to be missed so, with the cooperation of the BR crew, including Callum Macraild, the train, headed by a Class 37 diesel with two coaches, was stopped, reversed and performed a photographic run-past! *John Hunt*

In the West Highland line's centenary year, No 3442 *The Great Marquess* pilots No 2005 past Loch Dubh, between Beasdale and Lochailort, en route from Mallaig to Fort William on 9 August 1994. *John Hunt*

Left: No 62005 skirts the west end of Loch Eilt on 1 October 2007. *Andrew Bell*

Right: The 'K1', posing as erstwhile Fort William engine No 62012, pilots No 61243 towards Corrour near the end of the long climb up from Tulloch on 6 October 2002. *John Cooper Smith*

With Eigg and Rum as a backdrop, the loco accelerates away from Arisaig at Kinloid on 12 October 2014. *John Hunt*

Above: With Beinn Dorain in the background, No 62005 crosses the second viaduct in the 'horseshoe curve' on 6 May 2014. *Bob Green*

Overleaf: The snow-covered Ben More is reflected in the waters of Strath Fillan as NELPG's 'K1' No 2005 steams into Crianlarich on 5 November 1990 en route home to the North East after a season on the Road to the Isles. *Maurice Burns*

15 LOCO SHEDS AND WORKSHOPS

By the time NELPG engines arrived on the NYMR in the 1970s, the Group's members had worked on their locos at Tyne Dock, Philadelphia, Hartlepool, Thornaby and ICI Billingham. Thornaby was to play a vital role until 1975, providing a Teesside location close to the homes of many volunteers for the restoration of locomotives. This chapter tells of the determination of NELPG volunteers to both provide covered accommodation at Grosmont and once again to find a Teesside overhaul and restoration base, both vital for keeping engines steaming into the future.

Above: An early working party is seen with the 'J27' at Tyne Dock in December 1967, with the 'Q6' and No 69005 beyond. *Maurice Burns*

Right: At the NCB Philadelphia works, Co Durham, a NCB fitter adjusts the safety valves during the first steaming of No 65894 under NELPG ownership on 15 November 1968. *Maurice Burns*

The 'J27' and 'Q6' stand side-by-side in the Thornaby roundhouse after the first steaming of the 'Q6' by NELPG volunteers on 18 October 1969. *Maurice Burns*

This is the forlorn sight at the south end of Grosmont Tunnel, where there was once a turntable where the large bush is growing, and with Tunnel Cottages on the right. This was the site of the NELPG-inspired locomotive repair shed, eventually constructed by the NYMR. *Maurice Burns*

Grosmont Locomotive Repair Shed

When the NYMR started, the only covered accommodation for rolling stock was Grosmont Tunnel. The NELPG set up a sub-committee to find ways of creating a shed at Grosmont, but, with the aid of a grant from the English Tourist Board, the NYMR took over the financing of what is now the repair shed within today's Grosmont Motive Power Depot. NELPG funds were utilised to purchase tools and machinery including a radial drill and lathe from Heaton depot. These were

The shear legs at Tweedmouth in March 1969, clearly showing the restricted location that hampered dismantling of the huge frame and its loading onto rail wagons. The road crane used to lift them is hidden behind the wall. *Maurice Burns*

delivered by rail on the Whitby pick-up – a freight train that, at the time, ran from Tees Yard to Whitby several times a week.

Locomotive shear legs were used to lift engines, so that wheels and axles could be rolled out for repair. Once a common sight in locomotive sheds throughout the North East, with the end of steam operations they were quickly scrapped. The last set, located at Tweedmouth, was offered for sale in January 1969 but the purchaser was to be responsible for dismantling. The NELPG was just two years old at this time, and its volunteers, with an average age of 23, had probably

The shear legs in use at Grosmont to remove a driving wheelset from No 29 in October 1977. *John Hunt*

0-6-0ST *Salmon* stands at Deviation with wagons carrying the Tweedmouth shear legs ready for unloading in April 1969. On the right is Deviation signal box, which once controlled the junction with the Beckhole branch and which was demolished to make way for Deviation shed. The repair shed was to occupy the wasteland to the left of Deviation Cottages. *Maurice Burns*

never dismantled anything more than a push bike! Peter Hutchinson, Maurice Burns and Ian Storey paid a visit to Tweedmouth to see if the Group dare take it on. They had all seen shear legs before, but they looked twice as big now that they had to be dismantled.

The 40-ton-capacity equipment was so high that the 45-foot-high hydraulic cylinder came through the roof of the shed. The NELPG certainly wanted it, but the difficulty was that it was inside a building, and all parts had to be somehow dismantled and loaded onto rail wagons. How on earth could it be done? Ian Storey was reassured by a crane hire firm that dismantling could take place with the crane outside the building. An offer was duly put in and accepted by BR, so we now owned a huge set of shear legs standing at Tweedmouth! After a lot of careful thought, a crane was hired, the huge bolts were undone, and the heavy hydraulic cylinder and cross beam were lowered to the ground.

The 30-foot-high 'A' frames were more difficult. After demolishing part of the shed roof and undoing the foundation bolts, each frame had to be raised

8 feet by the crane to enable a rail wagon to go underneath it. In this process the crane alarm bell began to ring because of the total weight, and this was resolved by resting the crane jib on the building wall to take some of the weight! It took four weekends of work but all the parts were eventually loaded.

They were delivered to Grosmont on the Whitby pick-up train and, in 1973, were re-erected when construction of the repair shed began. The location of the shear legs within the repair shed was critical. Forward-thinking NYMR Civil Engineer Nigel Trotter said, 'Let's locate them for an 'A4' facing either direction,' and that's exactly where they are standing today! Within two years the repair shed structure was finished, complete with stores and a public viewing gallery.

Deviation shed

The Group still felt that there was a need for a separate locomotive storage shed at Grosmont. However, with no money this was but a dream. All this

The Grosmont repair shed in the course of construction, with the second track being laid, in 1973. Compare this with the picture on page 123. *John Hunt*

changed with the 1975 Stockton & Darlington 150th Anniversary celebrations. The NELPG not only turned out four locomotives for the Grand Cavalcade, but had a huge sales stall at a key exhibition location. What's more, the Group was beginning to generate income from railtours. As a result, the vision of providing a shed came a step closer. In 1976, after a long search through specialist classified adverts (no E-bay then!), a possible building of the right width and height was discovered, in deepest Hampshire, on the Longmoor Military Railway. Maurice inspected the building on his way from Gatwick Airport after a holiday flight. To save problems later, it was carefully measured and pictures taken, particularly of the bolted joints. The building had been used as a store and had been in the Far East during the Second World War. Some 210 feet long by 40 feet wide by 14 feet 2 inches high, it looked ideal.

With the help of the NYMR's Civil Engineer, Nigel Trotter, a site was sought at Grosmont, but there was a problem – nowhere was level. A site could only be created by moving an embankment and, sadly, demolishing Deviation signal box. All NYMR loco owners were asked if they were interested in buying a share of the available space. The NELPG wanted room

to house the combined length of the 'P3', 'T2', 'Q7' and 'K1' (the 'J72' was not purchased until after the shed was constructed), while Ian Storey wanted space for No 44767, Bob and Sylvia Jones for Lambton Tank No 5 and Ted Smith for No 31, an RSH 0-6-0T from NCB Ashington. With no other owners interested, some hard bargaining with the dismantling contractor saw the price for a nine-bay, 137-foot-long, shed, dismantled and delivered to Grosmont, agreed at £3,100. The remaining four bays were scrapped.

By 8 September 1976, only three weeks after the initial site inspection, the building had been dismantled and delivered as a 'flat pack' to Grosmont. What faced Maurice, who was the only one to see the building standing at Longmoor, and the team were hundreds of pieces of steelwork and cladding sheets, 18 windows, one roller shutter door and a mountain of huge bolts of different lengths but no drawings or assembly instructions! Demolishing Deviation signal box and the embankment, using a JCB and a tractor and trailer, the latter provided by Ian Storey, was a mammoth task over the winter of 1976/77. John Whitbread and Ian Storey operated the JCB successfully, while Alan Higgitt and Andrew Scott drove the tractor and trailer,

Deviation shed in the early stages of construction in 1978, with Ian Storey (left) and Toby Jones
at the top of the ladders and Rod Smith in the Coles crane lifting up the second roof truss. *Maurice Burns*

which, on at least one occasion, became totally stuck in the mud and had to be dug out! With the earth moved, Nigel Trotter and Andrew Scott set out the foundations and work began. Digging the foundation holes and shuttering for 24 foundations was no small task, with Alan Higgitt, Paul Smith, Dave Hancock and Peter Wrigglesworth lending a hand.

A major task was sorting the steelwork and identifying what went where, using the pictures taken at Longmoor. It was a mammoth jigsaw. The critical items were the roof trusses, each comprising 15 pieces of steelwork. As much pre-assembly and painting was done as possible, with the Brown family playing a key role. Eventually all steelwork was laid out and they were ready to go. As usual, the Group had no previous experience, but its members believed that they could do anything! With the aid of a Coles road crane operated by professional driver Rod Smith and a scaffold tower, they got under way.

The first day was a very special one, with a start made on erecting the steelwork,. With volunteers Ian Storey, Peter Smith, Ian Pearson, Neil Henderson, Paul Smith and others at hand, the newly painted columns went straight onto the foundation bolts, with shim packs for minor elevation adjustment. Then came to the first fully assembled roof truss, starting at the north end. By the end of day one, four columns, two complete roof trusses and connecting steelwork had been erected. It all fitted together without problems, was made vertical, then tightened up and made safe. Glancing back through Grosmont Tunnel as the group left for home, it was hard to believe that the huge aluminium painted structure had not been there when they had arrived in the morning! Steelwork assembly continued for many months, as volunteers were only available on Sundays. When the roller shutter doors and the windows were fitted, it started to look like a locomotive shed. With the windows re-glazed by Len Mayhew, the last major task outstanding was the cladding. None of those involved, particularly Dave Pennock, Richard Campbell and Bill Dobson, will ever forget the punching of every hole in the cladding to align the hook bolts to the roof steelwork. It was a job that seemed endless.

The NYMR Permanent Way team, led by Les Barwick, laid the first track into the building and, one Sunday in November 1978, the first locomotive, 'Q7' No 63460, was pushed into the shed by volunteers.

On a Sunday in November 1978 NELPG volunteers including Dave Freeman, Ian Pearson, Ian Storey, Paul Smith, Dave Husband and Peter Wrigglesworth symbolically 'push' the 'Q7' into Deviation shed, the first locomotive to be placed under cover. *Maurice Burns*

Completion of the rest of the track works, providing three roads, took until Easter 1982, and at last all of the NELPG's locomotives were under cover. This was such a proud moment after six years of toil.

NELPG Secretary Derek Hanson led the creation of a shed owner's agreement and a lease. The Owner's Group agreement with the NYMR listed the membership, financial contributions and responsibility arrangements and was for a term of 99 years at an annual rent of £1. Both documents were signed by all parties on 1 January 1979. The Group's dream of owning its own shed was now a reality. Bearing in mind the scale of the construction task undertaken by volunteers with full-time jobs and family commitments, the achievement was immense. All the technical problems were successfully overcome and, importantly, there was not one accident during the whole construction period.

Since completion, progressive improvements have been made. A complete lighting system was donated in

1980 with installation organised by Gordon Wells using an industrial contractor who undertook the job for just the cost of the materials. Concrete walkways were installed in 1983 and an air compressor provided.

To commemorate the NELPG's 25th anniversary the building was refurbished and all the cladding replaced, using funds generated by charging visitors 80p to access the Grosmont shed site. To mark the completion a commemorative brass plate was unveiled by NELPG President Bill Harvey on 16 June 1991.

Two years later a series of display cabinets, hand-built by Arthur Robinson and George Atkinson, were erected on the north-facing wall of the shed by Dave Whitfield. These contain panels telling the story of our locomotives past and present and a useful donation box. To this day these act as a focus for members of the public visiting the shed.

The NELPG's Great Central fish van was used as a store and workshop, later to be replaced by a much larger GWR 'Mink G' van until this, too, was

Prior to construction of the stores and inspection pit, this view inside Deviation shed shows, from left to right, Nos 65894, 3814, 60532 *Blue Peter*, 901 and 5. *John Hunt*

Derek Norris and Colin Smith in the new Deviation shed workshop on 21 February 2006. On the work bench is a 'Q6' valve, characterised by the single, broad valve ring (left). *Colin Smith*

NYMR PW staff Gerry Carter, Darren Lonsdale and Peter Smeaton fasten rails to the new pit on 19 May 2009. *John Hunt*

replaced by a two-storey concrete block construction inside Deviation shed. NELPG volunteers did all the necessary work to bring the new workshop up to ground floor level and the NYMR built the rest, to NELPG's design. Finally, a locomotive inspection pit under the middle road of the shed was installed during 2007/08, with both the workshop and pit being NELPG-organised projects.

ICI Wilton Teesside

The connection between the NELPG and petro-chemicals giant ICI Wilton, first established in 1985, proved to be fundamental to the Group's subsequent success. The 15-year partnership provided a free large workshop facility and a rail connection, paid staff salaries, provided free materials and craneage, and, crucially, provided access for 15 years to sponsored Government employment and training schemes. Such things do not just happen, so how did this estimated £1.2 million investment in the NELPG come about?

Between 1969 and 1975 the benefit of members on Teesside living very close to the engine restoration site at Thornaby was clear, with rapid restoration progress undertaken principally by evening working parties. These attracted a different type of volunteer from those who went to the NYMR on Sundays. The need to renew all of the roof stays of the 'K1', a major time-consuming task, led to a concerted effort to find a new Teesside locomotive overhaul base.

Sites at British Steel, near the Redcar Blast Furnace, and the old Furness Shipyard, were looked at, but the buildings were very primitive. A vital tip-off came from the late Alan Ramsay, that ICI was doing some small projects for Beamish Museum. Further research found the name and phone number of the ICI Wilton Teesside Operations Manager, Brian Caldwell. With some trepidation, a phone call was made direct to Brian, during which he was told about the NELPG's history and its need for a Teesside engineering base. This led to the first meeting on 20 June 1984, attended by Brian Caldwell and Dr Ian Pearce, Wilton Site Training Manager, during which Maurice Burns explained further, with photographs, and left a copy of the *North Eastern Revival* book. That did the trick – ICI was very impressed by the NELPG volunteers' achievements, and went away to think it over.

A phone call a few days later was to say that ICI could definitely help, and on 19 July 1984 a second meeting was arranged, where the NELPG was offered a choice of three different buildings at Wilton. No 5 depot was chosen because it had a 5-ton overhead crane, was a heated building, and had good washing facilities. On this date a simple handshake between Maurice, Brian and Ian established the vital partnership.

In 1984 the UK Government was running a training scheme, the Community Programme, to get unemployed people into work. Many charities benefited from this scheme to do landscaping, lay footpaths for the disabled, and rebuild abandoned canals. Their slogan was 'Unemployed people want it to work, the Government wants it to work, the community wants it to work but only sponsors can make it work'.

ICI suggested that the NELPG's locomotive restoration programme could provide useful projects. A scheme for the 'K1' was developed jointly by Dr Ian Pearce of ICI and Maurice Burns and Bill Dobson of the NELPG, which included estimated costs for wages, materials, work programmes, and lines of responsibility. ICI offered to pay the wages of a full-time scheme manager, Ken Thompson, in addition to providing workshop, insurance and medical facilities. The paperwork had ICI as the sponsor and the NELPG

as the patron, with work for the scheme's 14 full-time trainees and for NELPG volunteers being coordinated by Maurice Burns, assisted by Dave Pearson. The first scheme was submitted in August and approved shortly afterwards, with a start date of 1 October 1984.

The 'K1' rebuild was a resounding success for all parties, and a further scheme was submitted to overhaul the 'J72' No 69023 *Joem*, which arrived at Wilton as the 'K1' was nearly finished. This overhaul saw new water tanks, coal bunker, front tube plate and smokebox, all renewed at no cost to the Group. The scheme had an allowance for material costs per trainee hour worked, and in the case of the 'J72' this was more than enough for boiler tubes and motion repairs.

The manager of the joint ICI/NELPG Manpower Services Scheme was Ken Thompson (left), who managed the scheme workers and worked so well with NELPG volunteers for 15 years. Here he discusses the paint requirements for the 'J72' overhaul with Len Clarke in 1988; in the background stands the 'J72'. *Maurice Burns*

The MSC team poses in front of the 'J72'; Ken Thompson is third from the left. *Maurice Burns*

Inside No 5 depot, Wilton, the 'K1' is in a dismantled state on 20 November 1985. *John Hunt*

When *Joem* was ex-works from ICI it had cost NELPG absolutely nothing.

The ICI/NELPG partnership was a flagship scheme for the North East, and press and TV interviews were commonplace. On 16 May 1985 ICI Wilton had a visit from the Manpower Services Commission Director Geoffrey Holland and regional MSC directors. In true NELPG tradition they were each presented with a copy of *North Eastern Revival*!

The 'K1' and 'J72' had both been towed into the workshop on road vehicles through a low door at the north end. With the scheme extended, in 1987, to cover the repainting of *Bittern* as *Silver Link* and the overhaul of *Blue Peter*, ICI, at its own expense, decided to rail-connect the workshop. This was a major task but, when complete, it allowed the newly overhauled 'J72' to be used to shunt *Blue Peter* into the workshop in front of BBC cameras from the *Blue Peter* TV programme. The 'A2' saw regular visits from the programme and guests such as John Bellwood, Peter Townend (former shed master at King's Cross 'Top Shed'), and Dorothy Mather, widow of Arthur H. Peppercorn.

Further overhauls of the 'J27' and 'K1' in the late 1990s brought the NELPG's partnership with ICI to an end due to changing circumstances, as the company was selling off many parts of the site.

The whole collaboration with ICI was built on friendship and good working relationships between NELPG volunteers and ICI staff. Without the ICI connection to vastly improve the condition of each engine, the 'J72' and 'J27' would not have travelled throughout the UK, the 'K1' would never have reached Fort William, and running *Blue Peter* on the main line would have remained a dream rather than become a reality. Without doubt, the NELPG will always be indebted to the staff at ICI.

Hopetown Carriage Works

The ending of the NELPG's period at ICI Wilton, in August 1998, brought into sharp focus the need to retain the Teesside workforce, and an urgent search for new premises ensued.

The A1 Steam Locomotive Trust needed a building in which to construct its new-build locomotive *Tornado*. It found that the 1853-built, Grade 2-listed former Stockton & Darlington Railway Carriage Works at Hopetown, Darlington, was empty and ideal for its purpose. Darlington Borough Council owned the building and an agreement was signed in March 1995. Following refurbishment of the east end of the building, the Trust set up its permanent base there and brought the *Tornado* project to fruition.

In August 1999 it was Fred Ramshaw who spotted that the western end of the building was not in use. Following help from the A1 Steam Locomotive Trust and Dr Stuart Nichol, Curator of the Head of Steam Museum at North Road Station, Darlington, discussions with Darlington Borough Council took place that resulted in a long-term lease of the western section of the building to the NELPG being confirmed on 9 June 2001. The internal condition of the western end, with its windows boarded up, was just like a black

The refurbished Hopetown Works at Darlington from the outside in April 2016. *Maurice Burns*

This is the airy view inside Hopetown Works at Darlington in 2015, thanks to the new windows, with the 'J27' frames and the 'J72'. *Dave Pennock*

hole. A purpose-built tool and material store, toilet, shower room and mess room was constructed by Arthur Robinson and other contractors, at a cost to the NELPG of £25,000. Getting locomotive frames into the building was not straightforward, with the first set, belonging to No 63395, having to be craned in from Hopetown Lane. A more permanent solution was to connect the building to the existing track, with which the NYMR Permanent Way team assisted. There then followed a succession of overhauls of the 'J72', 'J27' and 'K1' frames, showing the success of a Tees Valley base for locomotive overhauls.

The whole building exterior had been in a poor state of repair for many years, but in 2015 Darlington Borough Council, owners of the listed building, replaced the windows and refurbished the exterior walls, causing a total and much welcome transformation.

As the NELPG enters its 50th anniversary year, the Group founders could never have imagined that in 2016 it would own Deviation shed at Grosmont on the NYMR, and have a first-class Tees Valley repair facility at Hopetown, Darlington.

16 THE CHALLENGE OF LOCO OVERHAUL AND MAINTENANCE

From the moment that the NELPG signed the cheque that bought 'J27' No 65894 on 1 December 1967, it was no longer just looking at photographs or the blackness of an engine's exhaust, but at 62 tons of scrap metal that was standing cold and rusty at Tyne Dock shed. Where does one start? With the successful purchase came the responsibility of deciding what to do next. Who will show leadership? Who has the engineering skills? Who will organise volunteers? All of a sudden, owning a steam locomotive did not look so easy. Did someone say, like a general election handout pledge, 'We intend to restore the engines to working order'? But where will the money come from to buy the new parts, or reconditioned old ones? The Group had no money! Finally, where was it going to store its prized possessions and do the restoration? The NELPG was at Tyne Dock and had nowhere else to go. During one of the first working parties there, while a member was wire brushing the boiler barrel for repainting a rivet head fell off. The first challenge of locomotive maintenance had arrived, bringing into sharp focus how poor the engines were mechanically at the end of BR steam. The Group had to progressively tackle this backlog.

As the earlier chapters have illustrated, NELPG members like a challenge. It started 50 years ago and continues to this very day. Challenges come in different forms in a volunteer organisation, but one of the hardest is that of locomotive maintenance, in particular finding the volunteer who has the engineering skill and is willing to take full responsibility for one, or all, of the locomotives. In the late 1960s the North East had a strong traditional engineering base and the BR fitters and boilersmiths were still on hand to answer questions and give advice. Early NELPG volunteers had to learn fast – and they did. The Group was fortunate that on the Committee there were two people just out of their engineering apprenticeships, Peter Hutchinson and Maurice Burns, (who subsequently became Technical Secretary, then CME), both then aged 22 and enthusiastic about getting stuck in and taking responsibility.

The first restoration work in the early 1970s was to get the engines into good working order and to fit vacuum brake equipment at minimum cost. The Group had learned re-tubing techniques on the 'Q6' in 1969 and had renewed all the small tubes on the 'K1' in 1973. Copper lacing in place of rivets on the copper flanges came next, as did renewal of side stays. There were just two stay breakages in the first 15 years, before worn heads of these components made renewals commonplace – but what about future maintenance and repair? When restoration was complete and the 'Q6', 'J27' and 'K1' were handed over to the NYMR, it was on the basis that it was the Railway's responsibility to do all the maintenance work and pay for it. The NELPG could have left those arrangements as they were, and sat back, with the likelihood that when the engines were due for major overhaul again, they might end up out of use and decaying in open storage for some time. Equally, the NYMR realised that it had neither the manpower resources nor the finance to service these big engines due to other demands for funds. A meeting of minds resulted in two types of hire agreement – one for NYMR-maintained engines and the other for owner-maintained engines, where the latter would be paid a sum per mile that would be index-linked. The NELPG Secretary, Derek Hanson, did a thorough job of drafting the agreement with the initial rate calculated at 60 pence per mile (£8.00 in 2016 values), accepted by the NYMR. This change of responsibility, signed on 1 January 1979, would have huge long-term volunteer and financial implications for the NELPG, because if the engines were not available for traffic they would not earn a penny. However, in looking back over the history of 50 years, this major decision by the NELPG to be in charge of the destiny of its own engines was surely one of the most significant made by the Committee. History shows that NELPG engines have, by and large, been in regular use, not only for NELPG members to enjoy, but also making an important contribution to the NYMR steam motive power requirement. The NELPG and the NYMR have both been winners!

One of the first major full mechanical rebuilds, brought on by banging axle boxes, was on the 'Q6' in 1981. These components were so bad that the Group had to go back to first principles – something it had not done before – of determining the exact relationship between the driving axle and the cylinders. It was during this complex rebuild, with Maurice Burns and Mike Oliver taking the lead, that Richard Campbell, a man with a keen eye for detail, became involved. When trying to check the length of the side rods, to ensure we had got the axle centres right, he found that the left side rod was a different length from the right by about an eighth of an inch. He made an eccentric bush to solve the problem. It was also at this time that Bill Harvey, former shed master at Norwich, who had written a book on steam locomotive restoration, offered his help. As a result, Bill offered to reset the valve gears on the 'Q6' and instruct others in the skill.

Sometimes, though, an engine will drive you mad! The 'J27' did that in the 1980s, when, after a successful boiler overhaul by volunteers at Grosmont, the axle boxes let us down and ran hot. When working with 60-year-old engines, with limited funds and different parts not in good condition, you have to patch them up as best you can. However, no matter what was done, the hot box problem did not go away. Drastic action was required, so the engine was moved to the relative quiet of the Stephenson Museum on North Tyneside, where a back-to-basic-principles approach, as on the 'Q6' earlier, was adopted, with Richard Campbell taking the lead. With his attention to detail, the problem was sorted for good.

After the last overhaul at Thornaby in 1975, all maintenance from that date was carried out at Grosmont. However, during this period the NELPG was somewhat distracted by the building of Deviation shed, so locomotive maintenance was minimised during the construction phase. In the 1980s we renewed the tyres on the 'K1' at British Steel, Rotherham, which was, at the time, a major task. The 'Q7' restoration was carried out entirely at Grosmont with a full boiler re-tube being done by NELPG volunteers, and once again Richard Campbell was heavily involved with the axle box work.

By 1984 the 'K1' needed new crown stays in the firebox. This forced the need to find a Teesside base, so to do this the NELPG formed its partnership with ICI, during which Group volunteers renewed all the roof stays. This task had never been done before by the NELPG, or indeed by many volunteer-run societies. This first overhaul at ICI, in conjunction with the Manpower Services Commission (MSC) scheme, brought the condition of the 'K1' to a new level, where the possibility of it operating from Fort William was realised for the first time, and volunteers loved it!

'J72' No 69023 Joem was the next engine through the superb ICI workshops, where, with the full support of the MSC scheme, new side tanks, bunker and smokebox were fabricated; and ICI donated a new front tube plate. The end result was a new locomotive, whose restoration actually cost nothing. This work enabled it to go on hire to other railways, throughout the UK, and in doing so it collected a Steam Heritage award.

By the late 1980s the Fort William operation was becoming a regular feature, but it almost stopped completely in 1988 because there were no available engines, and it coincided with the 'K1' needing a full retube. The engine had been on the SRPS Santa specials around Edinburgh until 13 December 1987, but when it returned to ICI Wilton just before Christmas volunteers formulated a plan to save the Fort William operation. This involved ICI agreeing that the NELPG could use its locomotive shed, rather than No 5 depot, which was full, and attempting to do a full boiler retube in 14 weeks. This, and other mechanical work, led to volunteers working on some part of the engine every day of the week for that period. The task got off to a good start over the Christmas holidays, when all the boiler tubes were removed, some of the enthusiastic volunteers, in particular Mike Oliver, getting rather black in the process! The determination to see the engine finished in time was achieved and the 'K1' returned to Fort William in 1988, thereby ensuring the continuation of the steam operation.

Old crown stays being removed by Bernie Lyth and Nigel Bill using a torque wrench. *Maurice Burns*

Showing just how dirty steam locomotives can be, Maurice Burns and Mike Oliver still manage a smile during the removal of 'K1' boiler tubes in December 1988! *Maurice Burns*

Keeping the MSC team of 15 full-time people busy and organised at ICI needed a constant flow of interesting tasks. However, a gap in available work for platers and welders saw a 'fill-in job' with the move of the 'Q6' tender from Grosmont to ICI for the fabrication of a new tender tank. As with *Joem*, there was no cost to the NELPG.

Chapter 13 told the story of the NELPG volunteers' biggest ever restoration job, on *Blue Peter*. The boiler overhaul, including a full re-tube, renewal of many broken stays (due to the earlier flue tube implosion at Dinting) and copper lacings in the tube plate flanges, were all top-quality work. These repairs gave no trouble over the 10-year life of the boiler ticket. In the 15 years that the NELPG used the ICI workshop at Wilton, it is estimated that the financial contribution by that company, in the provision and maintenance of workshop facilities, materials and

a full-time manager for the MSC scheme, amounted to £1.2 million.

In 1993 the 'K1' firebox sides were down to half thickness and therefore scrap. New copper side plates were required in the firebox and it was established that no one in the preservation movement had done this type of copper welding repair. The NELPG was extremely fortunate that member Ray Sowerby knew that British Petroleum (BP) in Hull had the necessary skills to do the job – and for free! A complex specification and scope of work was developed jointly

Following completion of its overhaul, *Blue Peter's* boiler is carefully lowered into the frames outside No 5 depot in August 1991. *Maurice Burns*

between BP and Chatham Steam. The latter company made a new throat plate and carried out re-staying and re-tubing for just £32,000 and, with the 'P3' boiler being done by the same contractor at a fixed price for £16,000, it was possible to negotiate a discount for the two boiler contracts!

The 'Q6' and 'J27' designs were generally as first built almost 100 years ago, and in NELPG care various design changes have been made, including improvements to the lubrication of axle boxes, crossheads and little-end brasses. The 'J27' has seen considerable change by replacing the 2⁵⁄₁₆-inch-broad ring piston valves with four ⁵⁄₁₆-inch-wide rings, for

repairs on a particular engine. Out of this was born the 1996 NELPG Locomotive Maintenance Policy. In 1998 Maurice Burns stepped down after 30 years as Technical Secretary and CME, and was replaced by John Graham. This event coincided with new challenges on different engines. Boiler work became increasingly more complex and many 'K1' overhauls were done by West Coast Railways at Carnforth, while the 'Q6' overhaul was done at Grosmont and Crewe. In 2016 the 'J27' overhaul was being carried out at Hopetown and Crewe, and this included casting, machining and fitting a new cylinder block, as well as a rebuilt tender.

For the management of locomotive costs, the

Maurice Burns and Richard Pearson trial-fit a rocker firebar in the new hopper ashpan for the 'J27'.with the aid of the overhead crane. *Maurice Burns*

greater steam tightness at the front end. The biggest change of all was to design and fit a hopper ashpan and full rocking grate using standard 'K1' rocker bars. This transformed the fire disposal at the end of the day's operation.

The increase in regulation and the tragic, and unnecessary, wheel-slip damage to *Blue Peter* at Durham led to more sharing of the responsibility. The NELPG had working party organisers at Grosmont for many years, but now it introduced the role of Locomotive Caretaker – a person who would, while working under the CME, be responsible for day-to-day

NELPG has traditionally kept a log of each locomotive's earnings and expenditure, and this gives a true picture of the high cost of keeping steam alive. Even when the 'K1' can earn a good six-figure sum from the 'Jacobite' season, the cost of repairs and overhauls soon eats up the finances. Keeping locomotives in full working order is not a cheap business. However, as an example of the scale of the work undertaken by volunteers, the overhaul of the 'K1' at Wilton between 1984 and 1986, even with the help of ICI and the MSC Scheme, still required a massive input of 7,500 voluntary man hours.

Just as important was the money raised by the

Group and earned from locomotive operations. This was used to purchase the specialist skills and materials beyond the capabilities of the volunteer force. Over the years, the Government's Railway Inspectorate, Network Rail, and the insurance companies, have all come to terms with the voluntary railway preservation movement and, as a result, the routines of essential maintenance have become well established. To keep nearly 100-year-old locomotives in steam requires the annual programme to become steadily more ambitious. Today, NELPG's management confidently commissions from volunteers or contractors work that would have been out of the question 50 years ago, as it could only be carried out in main railway workshops. In 1968, renewing the boiler tubes of a locomotive was seen as a major achievement. By contrast, re-tubing is now seen as routine. The 'Q6' has received a completely rebuilt tender top, the original having almost totally rotted away after an eventful 80-year life. Some of the more major work has included cylinders that have been re-bored, re-lined, or totally replaced with new. Axle boxes have been totally reconstructed, inner and outer fireboxes patched, new tube plates manufactured and new tyres fitted.

Volunteers who were involved with working

parties nearly 50 years ago, at Tyne Dock, would never have believed the complex work that is tackled today. During this time span there have been hundreds of volunteers: some may have only volunteered for a few years, whilst others, who were there at the start, are still going strong. NELPG would not be where it is today had it not been for those who have worked so hard over so many years. A key part of this success has been those who have taken responsibility, such as Working Party Organisers, Terry Newman, Bill Dobson and Paul Smith, and Loco Caretakers such as Fred Ramshaw, Richard Pearson, Alan Toomer, Chris Davison, Darrin Crone, Neal Woods and Paul Hutchinson. If there were awards, all volunteers should get one, including the supporting wives, partners and families. The volunteer contribution to locomotive maintenance has been a great success story and this book, Keeping North Eastern Steam Alive, must surely be seen as a lasting tribute to their efforts.

Some of the maintenance challenges are difficult to explain in words alone, so the following pictures – most of which have never before been published – graphically illustrate many of the parts and processes that constitute a steam locomotive and its repair.

In this dramatic view during the 1985 'K1' overhaul at ICI Wilton after its axle box overhaul, the rear driving wheel is replaced by volunteers including Doug Hardy, Eric Nott, Richard Campbell and Derek Shorten. *Maurice Burns*

Pictures showing a new 'K1' outer back plate being lifted into position at Carnforth on 28 March 2006 (above), and patching the outer firebox plates of the 'Q6' at Grosmont on 19 March 2004. (below) *John Hunt*

Dave Martin screws in one of the last roof stays into the firebox top during the 'K1' overhaul at ICI Wilton in 1985. *Maurice Burns*

Dave Donegan skillfully rivets over the 'K1' roof stays during the 'K1' overhaul at ICI Wiliton in 1985. *Maurice Burns*

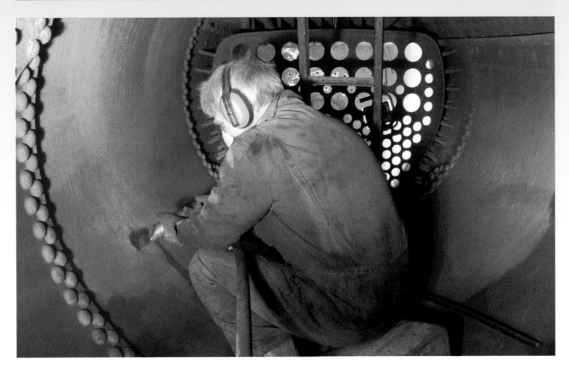

Fred Ramshaw needle-gunning inside the boiler of the 'K1' on 6 December 2005. *John Hunt*

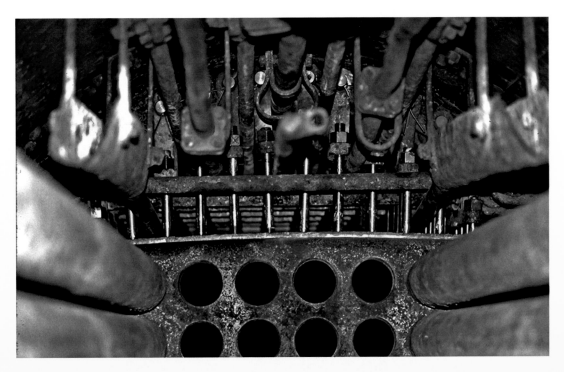

A rare view inside the same engine's boiler on 17 March 2006 looking towards the firebox tube plate, showing the large flue tubes, small tubes and newly fitted sling stays. *Maurice Burns*

With the 'K1' boiler
vertical and looking
into the firebox,
workmen from
British Petroleum
preheat the old
copper plates to
300 degrees C prior
to welding in new
copper sections in
June 1997. All this
work by British
Petroleum was
done free of charge.
Maurice Burns

A view into the
dome on the
top of the boiler
showing the
regulator valve.
John Hunt

Above left: Bernie Lyth, Bill Dobson and Mike Oliver fit a large flue tube to the 'K1' at Wilton in January 1986. *Maurice Burns*

Above right: Ian Storey, Paul Smith, Richard Campbell and Maurice Burns with boilersmith's tools inside No 4767's firebox on 19 April 1980 after a full retube. *Maurice Burns*

Left: These brand-new superheater elements will lie in the large 5-inch-diameter tubes, the upturned ball joints fitting into the superheater header. *John Hunt*

After a full re-tube of the 'K1' boiler by NELPG volunteers, Maurice Burns beads over the last flue tube with lighting assistance provided by John Tarn at Grosmont in 1981. *Maurice Burns*

This is one reason why a hydraulic test is carried out before a steam test: if there is a leak, you just get wet! John Whitbread attempts to tighten a washout boiler door on the 'Q6' as Paul Smith (left) and Dave Johnson look on in February 1973. *John Hunt*

Right: Bill Brown (left) and Dave Pearson guide the massive superheater header into position on the front tubeplate of *Blue Peter* using the overhead crane in No 5 depot. *Maurice Burns*

Below: There are several ways to lift engines in order to remove wheelsets; here the NRM's NER crane lifts the 'Q6' at Grosmont in June 1980. *John Hunt*

Left: Another way is by means of a wheeldrop. Here the leading wheelset of the 'A2' is raised back into the frames on the Thornaby wheeldrop in June 1995 following repair. *John Hunt*

Opposite page top: The 'K1's leading wheelset has its tyres reprofiled on the Thornaby ground lathe on 25 January 2006. *Richard Pearson*

Opposite page bottom: A new tyre, preheated by the gas burners, is fitted onto a 'K1' wheelset at Buckfastleigh on 25 November 2009. *South Devon Railway*

Below: Richard Campbell watches carefully as the trailing wheelset of the 'K1' is slowly raised back into position on the Carnforth wheeldrop on 6 January 2006. *John Hunt*

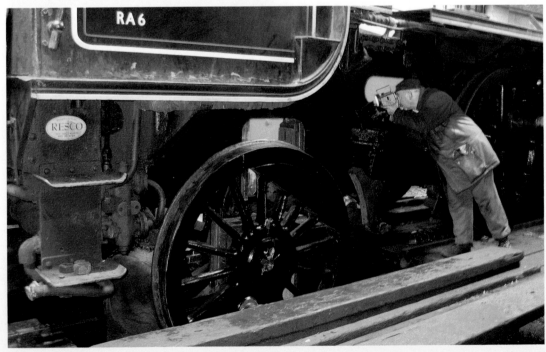

Above: A 'J27' axle box is machined by BR fitters George Hart and Peter Fawcett at Thornaby in 1970. *Maurice Burns*

Richard Campbell grinds the 'K1' axlebox horn faces true during an overhaul in the 1990s. *John Hunt*

Below: Maurice Burns and Mike Oliver refit a 'Q6' axle box in 1980. *Maurice Burns*

Opposite page top left: A cracked cylinder cover on the 'Q7' due to water in the cylinders.

Opposite page top right: The pony axle of the 'K1' is ultrasonically tested on 4 March 2004.

Opposite page bottom: Valve and piston bores become worn, especially in the middle, and have to be machined parallel, with the heads built up to compensate. Here, the right-hand valve of the 'J27' is bored by Bryn Engineering in April 2003. Once the bore has reached its limits, new liners have to be fitted. *John Hunt*

A new cylinder liner, reduced in size by being cooled to -196°C in liquid nitrogen, is fitted to the 'J27' by Dave Pinkney (BOC), Richard Pearson and Gordon Wells at ICI Wilton in 1995. *Maurice Burns*

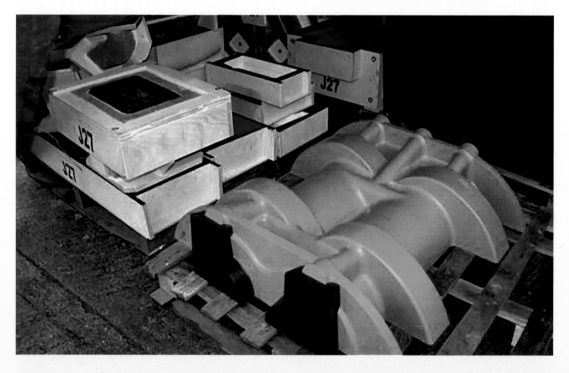

Before a new casting can be made, a complicated – and very expensive – set of wooden patterns has to be made; these are just some required for the 'J27' cylinder block. *Colin Smith*

The rough casting for the new cylinder block for the 'J27' on 1 July 2011.

Fred Ramshaw uses a block and tackle to lower the machined cylinder block into the 'J27' frames. *Colin Smith*

Left: Locomotive cylinders are one of the biggest areas of concern for the future, with all the engines requiring metal stitching to fractures at some point. The total renewal of the 'J27' cylinder block was a major project for volunteers to tackle at the Hopetown, Darlington, base. New skills were learned, with Neal Woods leading the team. Here is an example of metal stitching to repair a crack in the 'Q6' cylinder on 17 June 2010. *John Hunt*

Below: A view inside the tender water tank of the 'K1' on 21 January 2004, showing the baffle plates and part of the water level indicator. *Colin Smith*

Right: The chimney petticoat from the 'K1' is trial-fitted to a new spark arrestor, with the blower just visible through the mesh. In the background are secondary spark arrester screens.

Below right: Old and new 'K1' valve liners and valve heads: the grooves are for the valve rings.

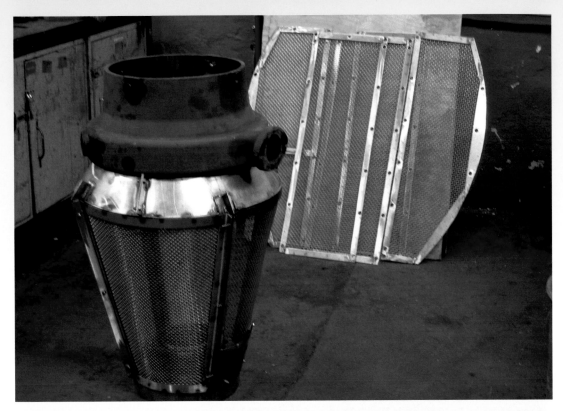

During the Durham incident the 'A2's left-hand leading driving wheel moved slightly on its axle, crushing the key between axle and wheel. The wheel had to be pressed off, the key ways machined true, a new key made and fitted, and the wheel pressed back on. Here, witnessed by Richard Campbell in the foreground, the wheel is being pressed back on at British Steel Redcar. *John Hunt*

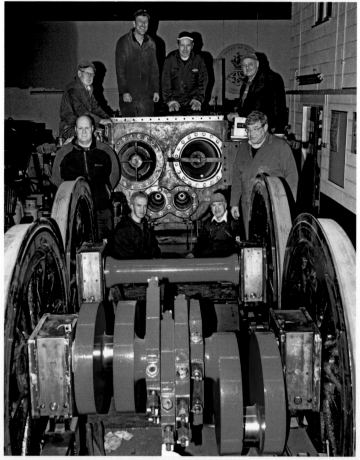

This picture, taken in December 2015 to mark the 50th anniversary of the closure of North Road works in 1966, shows part of the new Darlington works at Hopetown. Pictured are, back row: Terry Newman, Andy Lowes, Michael Chyriwsky, and Trevor Wilford (with *Blue Peter* badge); front row: Neal Woods (having his ear oiled), Paul Swainston, Steve Hyman, and Nigel Hall. In the foreground are the wheelsets off the 'J27', showing the webs for the two big ends and the four eccentrics. *Maurice Burns*

This view of the 'J27' inside the shed at ICI Billingham in early 1971 shows the tender after being filled and painstakingly rubbing down with 'wet and dry', and the engine in bauxite undercoat. *Maurice Burns*

Nigel Hall painting the inside of the 'K1' cab at Carnforth.

Kevin Hudspith applies black gloss paint to the 'Q6' tender inside Deviation shed.

Derek Hanson carefully lines out the 'K1' tender at Thornaby in April 1974. *Maurice Burns*

John Hardy and Peter Hutchinson, then just 23, sand down the wooden cab roof of the 'Q6' in the roundhouse of Thornaby in August 1969. Note the three link coupling from the 'Q6' a reminder of past days of hauling loose-coupled wagons that had no brakes. *Maurice Burns*

The 'Q6' cab with overhauled cab fittings, immaculate paintwork and varnished woodwork as originally restored in December 1969. This picture is of particular interest as it shows the cab fittings as the 'Q6' was originally designed in 1913 with the simple layout of regulator, two level gauges and two injector steam valves, plus the small hand wheel on the side of the right-hand injector steam valve. This small hand wheel controlled the steam brake for the engine and was the only brake on 600-ton loose-coupled coal trains – as the wagons had no brakes of their own. Before the 'Q6' left Thornaby in June 1970 this small valve was removed and a vacuum brake system installed. It is widely believed it was the fine attention to detail of the 1969 restoration shown in this picture by volunteers aged between 16 and 23 that greatly influenced the owners of the 'K1' to make the engine an outright gift to the NELPG.
Maurice Burns

Len Clarke carefully applies the blue shading to the name on 'A4' No 2509 *Silver Link* at ICI Wilton. *Maurice Burns*

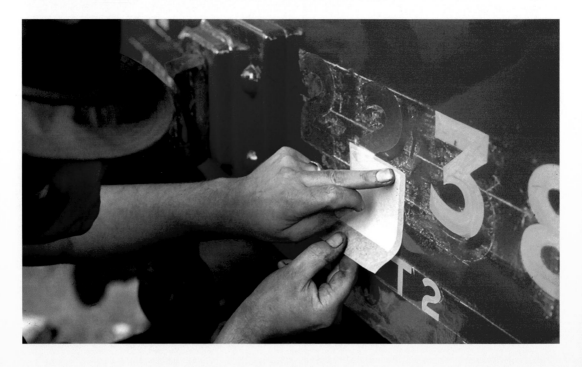

Len Clarke, having hand-painted the numbers on the buffer beam of the 'T2' with gold size, carefully applies the gold leaf in July 1975. *John Hunt*

In the atmosphere of BR's steam ban from 1968 onwards, Group members never dared raise their ambitions beyond operation on the NYMR. With the potential of an 18-mile run, this had always been a perfectly acceptable aim. The opportunity to embark upon main-line railtours in 1975 saw ventures further afield, and in recent years the NELPG's engines have increasingly found themselves at destinations never dreamed of in those early days, sometimes as a consequence of railtour operations, at other times on specific visits to help out or participate in events at other steam railway sites.

Several factors have led to the increase in these travels. First, the cost of road transport by low-loader has fallen relative to the income an engine can generate, and most lines are able to offload locomotives delivered by road. Second, the need to bring in outside motive power, either to counter shortages or to offer something

new, has increased. Perhaps just as important, today's more stringent regulations, which require boiler lifts and renewals at regular intervals, drive owners to find as much work for their engines as possible while they have valid boiler certificates.

Above: 'P3' No 2392 between Ingrow and Damens on the KWVR.

Left: Nos 2392, 29 and 4498 *Sir Nigel Gresley*, later to be joined by the 'Q6', on display in Newcastle Central station in April 1973 as part of the Newcastle Festival Exhibition. *John Hunt*

This new factor in managing a steam locomotive fleet has seen the NELPG's engines in operation or on display at numerous different locations, in addition to running on the main line. The following list shows the locations where NELPG locomotives have been steamed.

- Barrow Hill roundhouse   'J72', 'K1', 'A2'
- Black Country Museum, Dudley   'J72'
- Colne Valley Railway   'J72'
- Crewe Works Open Day   'A2'
- Darlington station '   K1'
- Dart Valley Railway '   'J72'
- Derwent Valley Light Railway   'J72'
- Didcot Railway Centre   'J72', 'A2'
- Doncaster Belmont   'A2'
- East Lancashire Railway   'J27', 'K1', 'A2'
- East Somerset Railway   'J72'
- Embsay & Bolton Abbey Railway   'J27', 'J72'
- Epping & Ongar Railway   'J72'
- Great Central Railway   'Q6', 'A2'
- Great Central Railway (North)   'J72'
- Hartlepool nuclear power station   'J72'
- Hull docks   'K1'
- Keighley & Worth Valley Railway   'J27', 'K1', 'A2'
- Lincolnshire Wolds Railway   'J72'
- Llangollen Railway   'J27'
- Locomotion, Shildon   'J27', 'Q6', 'K1', 'J72'
- Midland Railway Centre   'J72'
- Nene Valley Railway   'J27'
- Newcastle Central station   'J27', 'Q6'
- North Norfolk Railway   'J72'
- North Tyneside Railway   'J27'
- NRM, York   'A2', 'J27'
- Old Oak Common Open Day   'A2'
- Severn Valley Railway   'J72'
- South Devon Railway   'J72'
- Stockton station   'J27', 'Q6', 'K1'
- Swanage Railway   'J72'
- Tanfield Railway   'J72'
- Telford Steam Railway (Horsehay)   'J72'
- Thornaby Open Day   'A2', 'J27', 'J72'
- Tyseley   'K1'
- Weardale Railway   'J27'
- Wensleydale Railway   'J72', 'K1'
- York Railfest   'K1'

Road transport is regularly used to get locomotives to and from non-rail-connected locations. Here 'P3' No 2392 begins its journey from the NYMR to the NRM at York in September 1977. *Nigel Trotter*

No 2005 heads across Mytholmes Viaduct on the KWVR on 28 March 1982. *John Whiteley*

No 69023 climbs out of Mendip Vale on its way back to Cranmore on the East Somerset Railway in April 1991. *Maurice Burns*

Left: The 'J72' crosses the River Dart near Buckfastleigh on the Dart Valley Railway on 22 June 1991. *Maurice Burns*

Below: No 2392 skirts the Firth of Forth at Bo'ness with a train for Birkhill in August 1991. *John Hunt*

Opposite page top: No 2392 starts away from Berwyn Halt above the River Dee on the Llangollen Railway in September 1992. *John Hunt*

Opposite page bottom: Crowds flock to inspect *Blue Peter*, 'P3' No 2392 and *Joem* at Thornaby Open Day on 20 September 1992. Today all these buildings have been cleared away. *Maurice Burns*

No 2005 leaves the SRPS station at Bo'ness near Falkirk (with No 44767 in the background) on 8 November 1992. *John Hunt*

No 69023 arrives at Castle Hedingham on the Colne Valley Railway in August 1994. *Maurice Burns*

No 65894 enters Stoneacre loop with a ballast train from Bolton Abbey to Embsay
on 24 August 1998. *John Whiteley*

Also on the Yorkshire Dales Railway No 69023 passes impressively through Embsay station in September 1998.
Maurice Burns

No 62005 reflects the early morning sun at Burrs, with a train from Bury to Rawtenstall on the East Lancashire Railway, February 1999. *John Hunt*

No 60532 *Blue Peter* accelerates away from Loughborough on the Great Central Railway on 22 March 1999. *John Whiteley*

No 62005 is shunting in Hull docks on a photo charter in May 2000. *John Hunt*

Blue Peter keeps company with No 6024 *King Edward I* at Didcot depot in July 2000 during a visit to the Great Western Society. *John Hunt*

During the 1990's the NELPG's 'J72' No 69023 visited many railways in their hour of need and as a result many friendships were formed. Here, at a handover at the Swanage Railway in December 1991, their CME Martyn Ashworth shakes hands with the NELPG CME Maurice Burns watched by Chris Davison and Alan Toomer and the Swanage footplate crew. *Maurice Burns*

No 2392 runs between Frosterley and Stanhope on the Weardale Railway in February 2005. *John Hunt*

No 2392 is seen on display inside North Road Museum, Darlington, in May 2006. *John Hunt*

No 63395 heads south from Loughborough at Woodthorpe with a goods train on 31 January 2009. *Andrew Bell*

No 69023 'back home' where it used to work on the Derwent Valley Light Railway at Murton outside York on 21 July 2013. *Ken Snowdon*

Joem visits the Tanfield Railway during a coal train day on 12 September 2010. *Ken Snowdon*

No 69023 is seen again, waiting impatiently with the LNER 'quad-art' set at Sheringham
on the North Norfolk Railway on 13 March 2011. *Richard Pearson*

The following year the 'J72' is seen at North Thoresby on the Lincolnshire Wolds Railway
on 7 April 2012. *Les Nixon*

No 69023 is on Santa special duty between Bedale and Newton-le-Willows on the Wensleydale Railway on 23 December 2015... *John Hunt*

...and operating brake-van rides with 'A3' No 60103 *Flying Scotsman* on the rear, during the Shildon Shed Bash at Locomotion on 31 July 2016. *Maurice Burns*

18 CONCLUSION

The future – NELPG Junior Volunteers Ethan Humble, Noah Hunter, Dylan Bonnet, Tom Houseman, Rob Sowden, Henry Pritchard and Tom Noble pose in front of the 'Q6' after cleaning it at Grosmont on 9 April 2016. *Tom Noble*

Back in the halcyon days of 1966 it was unimaginable that the NELPG would be in the position in which it finds itself today. Entirely through voluntary efforts, those early ambitions were realised, to be rewarded in no small way by the outright gift of a third valuable locomotive, a magnificent gesture on the part of the previous owners, and the eventual acquisition of the 'J72'. The faith shown in the Group went on to be amply justified with the its contribution towards the restoration of Nos 5, 29 and 4767, the involvement in the Shildon celebrations, and the custodianship of the 'Q7', 'A4' and 'A2'.

In this book, NELPG members have tried to capture the story of their adventure. What stands out is the huge amount of effort that it has taken over so many years. It is therefore time to say a few words of thanks. The NELPG has always relied totally on its volunteer members. Skilled engineers, technicians, and just hard grafters, have always been crucial to keeping locomotives operational, by planning and executing their overhaul, restoration and maintenance, and preparing and running locos day by day. They are at the sharp end of the NELPG's work, and we need to thank them for their remarkable commitment to the cause. But behind the scenes there are more volunteers from a remarkable range of specialisms: everything from VAT returns and Gift Aid to legal services, social meeting planning, administration and fund-raising. Much of this administration is undertaken by the NELPG's Officers and Committee who, for most of the organisation's existence, have been Trustees of the Charity that the NELPG became. Since 1966, 60 members have served on the Committee and the buck has stopped with them. Needless to say, this has involved the spending of many long evenings around a committee table, usually far away from the Railway. More thanks are due to the very high percentage of members who have supported the work of the Group through donations over and above annual subscriptions – increasingly these days (but by no means only) through membership of the Patron scheme. No matter how much we earn from operations, there will always be a need for more if these ageing and increasingly expensive-to-maintain steam locomotives are to stay operating, and no matter how hard volunteer teams work they will always need cash for materials and for specialist services.

Thanks too go to people outside the Group. Since 1966 the NELPG has benefited from the support of non-members who respect its aims and its achievements: from those earliest days when sympathetic BR officers made things happen, or in some cases made sure that bad things didn't happen, as the Group sought to find its feet and acquire its locomotives. Today, individuals and companies of all descriptions continue to look helpfully on the Group's needs, from transport to graphics. Thanks are also due to a wide range of funding agencies – several private trusts and foundations, local authorities, the Heritage Lottery Fund and the PRiSM fund, originally of the Science Museum, now administered by the Arts Council. Without this huge constituency of engagement and support, the NELPG's locomotives would stop steaming.

Where next? No amount of support will help keep the vision alive if we don't bring on board a new generation of members and volunteers. The future is in the juniors and the families who support their involvement – some of these new members are pictured here. But it is also in people of all backgrounds and ages who want to join in – and there is always room for more. If you share the NELPG's vision that North Eastern steam should be kept alive, please go to www.nelpg.org.uk to find out how to join, and how to join in.

For the record, the following have held positions within the Group's administration between 1966 and 2016:

Presidents:
Alderman J. Burton (1967-69),
Bill Harvey (1983-94),
Andrew Scott CBE (2009 to date)

Vice Presidents:
Brian Hollingsworth (1969-2002),
Derek Marshall (1969-78),
Geoff Drury (1974-99),
Bryce Greenfield (1975-77),
Ian Storey (1984 to date),
John Bellwood (1988),
Peter J. Robinson (2013 to date)

Chairmen:
Bryce Greenfield (1966-71),
Ian Storey (1971-84),
Maurice Burns (1984-98),
John Hunt (1998 to date)

Treasurers:
Kevin Hudspith (1966-67),
Maurice Burns (1967-68),
John Richardson (1968-78),
Peter J. Robinson (1978-2012),
Ben Duncan (2012-13),
John Marsland (2013-15),
Richard Wheeler (2015 to date)

Secretaries:
Neville Stead (1966-68),
Maurice Burns (1968-69),
Cliff Cox (1969-70),
Chris Lawson (1970-73),
Derek Hanson (1973-80),
John Marsland (1980-81),
Dave Pennock (1981-88),
Dave Martin (1988-91),
Paul Hutchinson (1991-93),
Colin Hatton (1993-98),
Dave Martin (1998-2004),
Jackie Maples (2004-10),
Ben Duncan (2010-12),
John Hall (2012),
Chris Lawson (2012 to date)

Technical Secretary
Maurice Burns (1969-1989)

CMEs:
Maurice Burns (1990-98),
John Graham (2000 to date)

Other Committee members have been:

Steve Alder	Eric Nott
Nigel Bill	Mike Oliver
Ronnie Brown	Ted Parker
Richard Campbell	Richard Pearson
Michael Chyriwsky	Peter Potts
Eric Cox	Alan Priestley
Chris Cubitt	Peter Proud
Bill Dobson	Fred Ramshaw
Danny Fawcett	Stan Ritter
Kevin Gould	Peter Robinson
Clive Goult	Andrew Scott
John Hall	Colin Smith
Nigel Hall	Paul Smith
John Hardy	Chris Smyth
Peter Hutchinson	Alan Toomer
Paul Hutchinson	Gordon Wells
Dave Lewis	John Whitbread
Martin Lloyd	Dave Whitfield
Bernie Lyth	Peter Woodhouse
Terry Newman	

Over the last 50 years, and 295 issues, the sometimes onerous and unenviable task of keeping the membership abreast of developments by editing and producing *NELPG NEWS*, latterly six times a year, has been shared as follows:

1-12	Various Committee members including Cliff Cox and Maurice Burns
13-19	Maurice Burns
20-30	John Hunt
31	Chris Lawson
32-60	Andy Scott
61-72	Roger Melton
73 to date	John Hunt

For further information about the NELPG regarding membership, becoming a Patron, making a financial contribution, attending monthly social meetings or becoming an active volunteer, visit the NELPG website at www.nelpg.org.uk